CREATING GREAT
Town Centers
AND Urban Villages

Urban Land Institute

ULI–the Urban Land Institute
1025 Thomas Jefferson Street, N.W.
Washington, DC 20007-5201

Library of Congress Cataloging-in-Publication Data

Creating great town centers and urban villages.
    p. cm.
1. Architecture—Human factors. 2. Central places. I. Urban Land Institute.
    NA9053.H76C74 2008
    711'.4—dc22
                                        2008011750

ISBN: 978-0-87420-076-8

10 9 8 7 6 5 4 3 2 1
Printed in the United States of America.

© **Mixed Sources**
Product group from well-managed forests, controlled sources and recycled wood or fiber
www.fsc.org Cert no. SW-COC-002669
© 1996 Forest Stewardship Council

ABOUT ULI–THE URBAN LAND INSTITUTE

The mission of the Urban Land Institute is to provide leadership in the responsible use of land and in creating and sustaining thriving communities worldwide. ULI is committed to

☐ Bringing together leaders from across the fields of real estate and land use policy to exchange best practices and serve community needs;

☐ Fostering collaboration within and beyond ULI's membership through mentoring, dialogue, and problem solving;

☐ Exploring issues of urbanization, conservation, regeneration, land use, capital formation, and sustainable development;

☐ Advancing land use policies and design practices that respect the uniqueness of both built and natural environments;

☐ Sharing knowledge through education, applied research, publishing, and electronic media; and

☐ Sustaining a diverse global network of local practice and advisory efforts that address current and future challenges.

Established in 1936, the Institute today has more than 40,000 members worldwide, representing the entire spectrum of the land use and development disciplines. ULI relies heavily on the experience of its members. It is through member involvement and information resources that ULI has been able to set standards of excellence in development practice. The Institute has long been recognized as one of the world's most respected and widely quoted sources of objective information on urban planning, growth, and development.

PRINCIPAL AUTHORS

Prema Katari Gupta
Scholar in Residence
Urban Land Institute

Kathryn Terzano
Associate, Publications and Awards
Urban Land Institute

CONTRIBUTING AUTHORS

Michael D. Beyard
Senior Resident Fellow
ULI/Martin Bucksbaum Chair for
   Retail and Entertainment
Urban Land Institute

Anita Kramer
Senior Director, Retail and Mixed-Use Development
Urban Land Institute

Bruce Leonard
Principal
StreetSense, Inc.
Bethesda, Maryland

Sam Newberg
Writer
Minneapolis, Minnesota

Andrew Overbeck
Writer
Columbus, Ohio

Michael Pawlukiewicz
Director, Environment and
   Sustainable Development
Urban Land Institute

Dean Schwanke
Senior Vice President, Publications and Awards
Urban Land Institute

Jason Scully
Senior Associate, Publications and Awards
Urban Land Institute

Julie D. Stern
Writer
Falls Church, Virginia

Dorothy Verdon
Writer
Alexandria, Virginia

Nora Yoo
Project Associate
Urban Land Institute

PROJECT STAFF

Rachelle L. Levitt
Executive Vice President, Global Information Group
Publisher

Dean Schwanke
Senior Vice President, Publications and Awards

Adrienne Schmitz
Senior Director, Residential
   Community Development
Project Director

Nancy H. Stewart
Director, Book Program
Managing Editor

Lori Hatcher
Managing Director, Publications Marketing

James A. Mulligan
Associate Editor

Barbara Hart, Publications Professionals LLC
Kevin Harris, Publications Professionals LLC
Copy Editors

Betsy VanBuskirk
Art Director

John Hall Design Group
Book Design and Production

Jennifer Mineo
Design Assistant

Karrie Underwood
Digital Images Manager

Craig Chapman
Director, Publishing Operations

ACKNOWLEDGMENTS

A great many individuals contributed to this book, and we are indebted to them for their help, advice, and support. First and foremost, we would like to thank the many developers, architects, and planners who provided data, written materials, illustrations, and photographs. We are also grateful to many ULI members in the field who shared with us their ideas for this work. There were many wonderful and progressive projects that could not be included because of the space limitations of this small volume. In addition, we greatly appreciate the dedication and skill of the case study authors who crafted this information into meaningful narratives.

There are many to thank at ULI. First, we would like to acknowledge the immeasurable contribution of Adrienne Schmitz, whose guidance, patience, and creativity made this book a reality. Maureen McAvey, Bill Hudnut, Ed McMahon, Tom Murphy, Michael Beyard, and John McIlwain continue to be terrific mentors who were instrumental in the shaping of this project. Rachelle Levitt, Gayle Berens, and Dean Schwanke provided valuable guidance. Nancy Stewart lent her expertise in managing the book's production. Many thanks are owed to Betsy VanBuskirk, Kevin Harris, Barbara Hart, and John Hall for all their hard work. Others at ULI whose contributions we would like to acknowledge are Jason Scully, Matt Rader, and Rick Haughey.

A team of planning and development experts drawn from around the United States convened a workshop in Washington, D.C., in 2006 to distill principles of town center development. Those experts included: Chair Peter A. Pappas, Michael D. Beyard, Michael P. Buckley, Kevin R. Cantley, Leigh M. Ferguson, Robert J. Gibbs, Frank Gray, Phyllis M. Jarrell, Philip S. Lanzafame, Bruce Leonard, Gregg T. Logan, James A. Ratner, Charles "Terry" Shook, and Yaromir Steiner. Using those principles, ULI staff members Michael D. Beyard, Anita Kramer, Bruce Leonard, Michael Pawlukiewicz, Dean Schwanke, and Nora Yoo subsequently wrote a ULI booklet titled *Ten Principles for Developing Successful Town Centers*. We would be remiss not to mention the contribution of those experts and staff members to this book. The booklet is reproduced here as the chapter titled "Development Principles."

To anyone else who had a hand in this work and could not be mentioned in this limited space, we are sincerely grateful.

Prema Katari Gupta
Kathryn Terzano

Contents

Case Studies

CREATING GREAT

Town Centers
AND Urban Villages

INTRO
DUCTION

Community development patterns are evolving to suit people's changing needs. Today, more people are choosing a more pedestrian-oriented lifestyle and are turning to more sustainable ways of life. They value their limited free time and demand shortened commutes, more appealing surroundings, and a greater connection to their community. They envision living someplace where their children can walk to school, the park, and friends' homes. They yearn for and mull over a time when living near the corner store and knowing the neighbors by name was commonplace. They might also seek a more vibrant community than the one in which they currently live—a place where there is 24/7 activity. Such dense, walkable communities are not restricted to elusive places from the past or the most urban Manhattan neighborhoods. Those kinds of neighborhoods and places are being built today in the form of town centers and urban villages.

What Are Town Centers and Urban Villages?

A town center is an enduring, walkable, and integrated open-air, mixed-use development that is organized around a clearly identifiable and energized public realm. It is anchored by retail, dining, leisure, and vertically or horizontally integrated residential or office uses, typically combined with at least one other type of development, including hospitality, civic, and cultural uses. Over time, a town center should evolve into the densest, most compact, and most diverse part of a community, with strong connections to its surroundings.

Similarly, an urban village is a dense, self-sustaining, walkable community that has a strong residential component and includes a combination of retail, dining, leisure, and commercial uses—

Located in the Denver suburb of Lakewood, Belmar offers a pedestrian-oriented environment with the amenities of a downtown.

Photo by Frank Cruz, Continuum Properties

2

At the Woodlands, Market Street is part of a mixed-use town center that provides the north area of Houston, Texas, with a thriving urban core.

Walter Larrimore Photography

in short, a compact development in which people can live, work, and play. Urban villages are distinguished from town centers by having a higher intensity of residential development and a lower emphasis on retail uses.

Town centers and urban villages have only recently regained popularity, and their number has grown substantially over the past ten years. However, for more than half a century, suburbanization has been the dominant force in America's metropolitan growth and development. During this period, the nation's population has shifted dramatically, so that today more Americans live in suburbs than anywhere else. In fact, two suburbs—Mesa, Arizona, and Arlington, Texas—are now among the 50 largest cities in America, and the next census will likely include more suburbs.

As suburban populations have soared, along with jobs and shopping opportunities, many suburbanites have happily chosen to live independent of the older cities that form the core of their metropolitan areas. Many never visit the city except for an occasional concert, sporting event, or night on the town. At the same time, suburbanites are increasingly aware of the growing shortcomings of their own communities. They do not like monumental traffic jams, deteriorating suburban strips, obsolete enclosed shopping malls, an aging monoculture of single-family homes, and environmental degradation.

Outdoor seating and a fire pit provide a gathering place at Clipper Mill, an adaptive use project in Baltimore, Maryland.

Patrick Ross Photography

One consequence of the development patterns of the past 50 years is that there are few public places in suburbia where all segments of society can get together to interact, to celebrate, to stroll, to run errands, to protest, to sit and watch the world go by, or just to enjoy day-to-day living. The reason: these types of places are typically found in and around downtowns, and downtowns were generally not part of the suburban dream. From the beginning, suburbs revolved around private pleasures such as backyard barbecues, football practice, country clubs, and stay-at-home moms. Downtowns were considered anachronisms at best. At worst, they were considered to be filled with issues to avoid such as crime, deterioration, poverty, and people who are different. As a result, suburban downtowns seldom got built.

Shopping was also designed to be different in the suburbs. Gone were the streetfront stores that were intimately connected with the life of the community in cities. That eclectic mix of new and old, mom-and-pop stores, and personalized service was replaced by more standardized, no-hassle environments with predictable chain stores, mass market appeal, and plentiful parking in an impressive array of sophisticated shopping center types, formats, and environments. Gone too were opportunities to walk to the corner store, the movies, the library, the town square, or the local café, because land uses were designed to be separate. And many of those developments and streets had no sidewalks, making it unsafe to walk anywhere. Areas of town were set aside for residential, commercial, and industrial uses, eliminating the possibility of living in a loft over top of the local bookstore or deli or of living over your business if you were an entrepreneur. The separation of uses made sense when industry dominated cities, but this economic condition is no longer the case. As a result, town center and urban village concepts are flourishing today.

What Are the Changing Attitudes?

Today, as cities and downtowns are changing, suburban attitudes toward them are also changing. Seven factors are principally responsible:

☐ **THE TYPICAL SUBURBANITE HAS CHANGED.** No longer is suburbia dominated by white, middle-class couples with children. Today, the suburbs are often as diverse—in terms of race, household size, culture, income, age, sexuality, and lifestyle—as the cities they surround. This shift suggests that different development solutions are needed to meet contemporary needs—such as a range of housing types and shopping options to accommodate all lifestyles at different life-cycle stages.

☐ **THE PROBLEMS ASSOCIATED IN PAST YEARS WITH DOWNTOWNS,** especially crime, deterioration, and visual blight, have dissipated. Today, the downtowns of many cities are desirable locales again.

☐ **RELENTLESS, LOW-DENSITY SUBURBAN DEVELOPMENT PATTERNS** that require a car to go anywhere are unsustainable, given the projected scale of suburban growth and the increasing cost of oil, land, and infrastructure. People are increasingly aware of this, and many are willing to change their lifestyle as a result.

☐ **THERE IS A POWERFUL DESIRE IN SUBURBIA** to recreate the sense of community and connectedness that was lost as metropolitan areas grew so quickly in the past few decades.

☐ **SUBURBANITES, LIKE ALL PEOPLE, HARBOR A SIMPLE DESIRE** for more convenience in their busy lives.

☐ **SMART GROWTH MOVEMENTS ARE GAINING POPULARITY** as voters begin to realize the hidden costs of current suburban development practices.

☐ **SUBURBANITES NOW ACTIVELY SEEK A DOWNTOWN ENVIRONMENT,** even if they do not want to live downtown. They want the amenities of a sophisticated urban lifestyle, and they are drawn to these environments for shopping, visiting, and leisure activities.

As suburbs age and take on many of the characteristics of cities, they need to evolve as cities have evolved for millennia: creating walkable environments, broadening housing choices, offering mobility options, mixing land uses, selectively increasing densities, enhancing their civic and cultural presence, increasing diversity, and redeveloping obsolete and underused properties to provide more cosmopolitan environments and amenities. This change is already beginning to happen. Downtowns—those places that many suburbanites have avoided for decades—are one of the last missing pieces of the suburban development puzzle. Now being set in place from coast to coast, they are called town centers and urban villages.

Numerous obstacles can retard the natural evolution of suburbs into more livable and sustainable communities that include town centers and other urban amenities: NIMBYism (Not In My Back Yard) is at the forefront of actions to short-circuit suburban evolution. By working with com-

6

munity members at every step of the planning process, projects have a greater chance of succeeding, and residents are more likely to look favorably upon developments that they had a hand in
creating. When Bethesda Row in Bethesda, Maryland, was first proposed, many residents were
concerned about its potential influence on the community, fearing that the project would drive local
retailers out of business and replace them with the same national retailers that could be found at
any mall. Federal Realty—the developer of Bethesda Row—addressed those concerns by meeting
with local residents to discuss their ideas for the development and by demonstrating through its
leasing strategy that their fears were unfounded. Indeed, Federal Realty has managed to attract an
interesting mix of local, regional, and national retailers that together generate considerable customer traffic while still providing a unique shopping experience.

Assembling and developing land parcels that are suitable for town centers is sometimes another
obstacle in the creation of town centers, because complex and sophisticated partnerships between
the community and private landowners can come into play. Zoning and subdivision regulations
must often be modernized to allow for mixed uses because, historically, zoning has served to separate residential, commercial, and industrial uses. However, mixing commercial, residential, civic,
and cultural uses raises unusual development challenges and adds costs to the development process. And integrating contemporary, large-format retail space and adequate parking into an urban
context is difficult. But communities throughout the country are succeeding, and thriving town
centers and urban villages are being created.

**Legacy Village—
located on the
periphery of
Cleveland in
Lyndhurst,
Ohio—was one
of the first open-
air, mixed-use
developments in
the area.**

*Courtesy of
First Interstate
Properties, Ltd.*

7

Town centers in themselves

represent a hot trend in both retail and residential development. In the greater Washington, D.C., metropolitan area alone, more than 20 town centers have been built, are under construction, or are in advanced stages of planning. The Los Angeles, California, area is home to another dozen town centers. Suburban Cleveland, Ohio, has at least three town centers that have already been built: Crocker Park in Westlake, Ohio (see case study on page 92); Legacy Village in Lyndhurst, Ohio; and First & Main in Hudson, Ohio. Although the traditional town center model—with its mixed uses, walkability, and live/work/play amenities—was until recently seen as outdated, this view is now changing as developers and community members alike see the virtues of the new town center and urban village projects.

Developers are increasingly proficient at building on both brownfield and greyfield locations, and they are willing to pay for the rehabilitation of the site to gain a more desirable location. Some of those locations exist near subway stations, regional rail stations, and bus terminals—making multimodal designs more viable. Like traditional town centers, the new projects are being designed to connect with the existing community, to have the flexibility to grow and change over time, and to allow a diverse expression of architectural and design styles. Some town centers even create an imagined urban history through storyboarding, where parts of the development are given more aged looks to show how a town center may have evolved over time.

Civic anchors, such as libraries, theaters, and city halls, are being incorporated into town centers and urban villages more and more. Grocery stores, hardware stores, and other providers of daily needs are becoming part of many plans. Offices and hotels are also being included. To develop this

Mockingbird Station is a mixed-use development that is built adjacent to a station on the light rail line of the Dallas Area Rapid Transit.

Courtesy of RTKL Associates Inc.

8

range of uses, private sector developers are more frequently partnering with local government, as well as with nonprofit organizations. Those partnerships allow projects to be built that may not have otherwise been feasible. In the case of Issaquah Highlands, a planned community near Seattle, Washington, that includes a town center, the development was the result of a public/private partnership among Port Blakely Communities, the city of Issaquah, King County, and the state of Washington. This partnership was necessary for several reasons, including the growth-limiting regulations that were set by King County, as well as the considerable amount of public infrastructure (schools, medical facilities, emergency services, and an off-site highway connector) that was required. In Downtown Silver Spring, Maryland, a public/private partnership helped develop an area when several earlier, private sector plans had failed (see case study on page 100).

Strategic Site Selection

Although many early town centers—including Reston Town Center in Virginia, Princeton Forrestal Village in New Jersey, and Easton Town Center in Columbus, Ohio—were built on greenfield sites, the latest generation of mixed-use village developments includes an increasing number of projects built on infill sites or reclaimed land. Brownfields, which are defined by the U.S. Environmental Protection Agency as "abandoned, idled, or under-used industrial and commercial facilities where expansion or redevelopment is complicated by real or perceived environmental contamination," have become desirable locations for town center and urban village development, particularly as many North American cities now are actively repositioning their economies from industrial to postindustrial.

Even though the biggest hurdle in redeveloping brownfield sites into town centers or urban villages is the perceived risk of contamination, the advantages supporting the trend are numerous. Energy

The Food Hall at Victoria Gardens in Rancho Cucamonga, California, demonstrates how storyboarding was used in the project's design.

Courtesy of Forest City

Port Credit Village—an infill community on the shore of Lake Ontario, south of Toronto—occupies a former brownfield site.

Photo by Philip Lengden

and transportation costs, worsening traffic congestion, and long commuting times have increased the desirability of centrally located and easily accessible brownfield sites. Often brownfields are riverfront or waterfront sites, making reclamation particularly desirable to a community as this valuable amenity is given back. The original uses of such sites were frequently important economic generators that spurred adjacent residential development; this history can make redevelopment particularly interesting. Redevelopment of such sites is consistent with smart growth policy goals and makes use of existing infrastructure. The financial toolkit available for the conversion of contaminated land into taxratable land is increasing, and the renovation generally includes federal, state, and local programs such as grants and revolving fund loans. Recent examples abound and include Atlantic Station in Atlanta, the East 29th Avenue Town Center in Denver's Stapleton airport redevelopment (see case study on page 110), and SouthSide Works in Pittsburgh (see case study on page 176).

Another such example is Port Credit Village, a 27.2-acre (11.0-hectare) urban village built on the brownfield site of the St. Lawrence Starch Company's former factory on Lake Ontario, 20 minutes from downtown Toronto, Ontario, Canada. The site was occupied for more than 100 years by the St. Lawrence Starch Company, which operated a cornstarch and syrup plant known as "the Starch Works" from the late 1890s until 1990. The site was contaminated with industrial waste that had to be remediated before development could take place. The site also was covered with the foundations of the old factory buildings, which had to be demolished. In 1998, the FRAM Building Group and Slokker Canada saw an opportunity to redevelop the site as a mixed-use project that would create new urban experiences for Port Credit residents, as well as reestablish important links to the existing urban fabric and the waterfront.

Completed in 2005, Port Credit Village's three condominium buildings, commercial buildings, and townhouses contain 410 residential units, including 18 live/work spaces; 30,000 square feet

(2,800 square meters) of retail and office space; and 1,300 parking spaces, most of which are located underground. In addition, the city of Mississauga developed the 4.4-acre (1.8-hectare) St. Lawrence Park, which includes a large public square, a 1,500-foot-long (460-meter-long) landscaped waterfront promenade, and historic artifacts from the site's industrial days. Artifacts from the starch company's factory, as well as its original administration building, have been preserved as reminders of the site's industrial heritage. Port Credit Village joins two formerly separated sides of Port Credit—a 170-year-old village within the city of Mississauga—connecting it with a restored waterfront and providing a gentle transition from high-rise development on the west to single-family housing on the east.

Transportation Choices

Multimodal streets—increasingly known as "complete streets"—are defined as streets that can comfortably accommodate multiple modes of transportation, including public transportation, pedestrians, and bicycles, as well as private vehicles. Multimodal streets accommodate more trips by more people in the same amount of space by improving transit and providing better pedestrian and bicycle facilities. All types of transportation are considered to be equally important, thus helping mixed-use development become successful, as well as reducing traffic congestion.

Town centers and urban villages are ripe for multimodal streets because those developments frequently cluster together uses such as residences, stores, offices, schools, and recreation centers. Many people value living in or visiting a community where walking and cycling are safe, pleasant, and common and where everyday errands such as shopping and taking children to school or parks are convenient. When they are provided a variety of options, people can then decide which mode of transportation serves them best for a given activity. A range of options also means that people can change their minds according to their inclination, energy, available time, and other personal factors on that day for that activity, such as bicycling to work one day and taking the bus to work another day.

Compact, mixed-use land development places employment and retail activities in closer proximity to living areas with designs that favor nonmotorized transportation and transit access. Benefits of such developments include automobile trip reduction, decreased road congestion, and a lowering of urban area vehicle miles of travel. The new developments do not exclude the automobile; instead, they favor pedestrian and transit activity. The convenience of the car and the opportunity to walk or use transit can be blended in an environment with local access for all the daily needs of a diverse community. Bus or rail transit service would be available, providing viable transportation alternatives to shopping and employment activities in other communities and areas.

Nonetheless, adequate convenient parking is essential to the success of retail developments and is necessary for office and residential uses as well. Cars are the most important part of our transportation system, and many people rely on their cars to get to stores, to get to work, and to get home. Accordingly, an efficient, well-designed parking system must be planned at the beginning. It is especially important that parking be shared among uses. Thus, parking that is used by office workers during the day can be used by residents or theatergoers at night. Well-managed, convenient, and visible parking facilities contribute greatly to a town center's appeal. It is important to remember, however, that one of the primary benefits of a dense town center is to keep automobiles in their place—supporting, not dominating. If cars and parking dominate the town center, it will not achieve the overall livability and pedestrian friendliness that make the town center concept work.

The size of a town center and the amount of parking needed are based on the size of the target market. Is the town center appealing to a regional market, a community market, or perhaps just a neighborhood market? The bigger the market is, the higher the density threshold for the project. In any case, the goal is to build to the threshold of density that is necessary to attain a critical mass for that town center. For town centers that are already built, achieving this goal means reworking the master plan to allow for more dense development.

Within walking distance of a subway station, the Market Common in the Clarendon section of Arlington, Virginia (near Washington, D.C.), supports multimodal choices.

Courtesy of McCaffery Interests, Inc.

Town centers and urban villages can encourage a multimodal approach to transportation by the following:

☐ **PROMOTE BICYCLE USE** and comfort by designating bicycle routes throughout the development with bike lanes and bike facilities.

☐ **LEND SUPPORT FOR PUBLIC TRANSIT USE** through transit amenities, and identify streets where physical improvements can be made to enhance transit service.

☐ **PROVIDE TRANSIT AMENITIES** such as bus shelters, information, and bulb-outs.

☐ **SUPPORT PEDESTRIANS** through wide sidewalks (10 feet to 20 feet [3 meters to 6 meters]), landscaping, crosswalks, medians, and curb extensions.

Public Participation

Increasingly, the development of successful town centers and urban villages involves a public/private partnership. As public sector officials increasingly embrace the tenets of smart growth and compact development, the encouragement of mixed-use town center development becomes a public policy goal. As a result, municipal officials will want to participate in the mixed-use development.

The public sector's motivation for getting involved with the development of town centers and urban villages varies widely. Members of the public may view getting involved as a way to create both an identity and the gathering places within their community, and they may seek a focal point where residents can visit either for community events or just to enjoy day-to-day living. Other times, they may be motivated by economic development: job growth and the expansion of the municipal tax base.

A public partner can also offer a wide range of tools that can make an otherwise pie-in-the-sky project both feasible and profitable to a developer. Most obviously, the municipality can favorably change land use regulations, which often favor single-use, car-oriented development and which implement mixed-use or performance-based zoning. Rules can be changed to allow stacked uses, narrow streets, lower parking requirements, higher densities, and pedestrian circulation. Additionally, the city may provide public financing tools for a desirable mixed-use project. Tax increment financing may be used to finance infrastructure improvements and structured parking. Other forms of support include land write-downs, equity investments, soft second loans, and property tax abatements. The power of eminent domain may be used to obtain hold-out properties that impair land assembly. New parks and other improvements may be funded by a municipality's capital budget or, perhaps, a local foundation. Finally, the public partner can place civic uses—libraries, schools, post offices, performance centers, museums, and other institutional and cultural facilities—within the town center so those uses can lend the project a sense of legitimacy and authenticity that might otherwise be unobtainable.

In the case of Silver Spring, Maryland, which is located in Montgomery County inside the Washington, D.C., beltway, the county sought a catalytic project that would revitalize Silver Spring's

core and would spur further redevelopment. In the 1980s, a four-block site known as the Silver Triangle Urban Renewal Area was condemned and assembled, but several attempts to redevelop the site, including a planned "American Dream" megamall, failed.

However, in 1997, the county entered an agreement with PFA Silver Spring, LC—a partnership of Washington, D.C., metropolitan area–based firms Foulger-Pratt, Argo Investment Companies, and the Peterson Companies—to negotiate a joint development plan for a mixed-use project on the urban renewal area site. In April 1998, the county and PFA signed a general development agreement that specified the conditions under which the county and PFA would work together to develop a mixed-use urban entertainment and retail center incorporating the existing historic structures and featuring a traditional street format punctuated by urban plazas. The agreement between PFA and the county called for $189 million of private investment for the retail, office, residential, and hotel components. The county agreed to provide $132 million for acquiring land and demolishing the existing structures, for building two public parking garages, for streetscaping, for restoring a

Participation by both private and public entities was key in the development of Downtown Silver Spring in Silver Spring, Maryland.

R.C. Kreider Studios, Inc.

historic theater and the façade of a historically significant shopping center on the site, for creating a live performance theater, and for constructing a civic building.

In 2006, the mixed-use destination of Downtown Silver Spring was realized, which has since been a catalyst for further redevelopment in adjacent areas. When asked if it could duplicate Downtown Silver Spring in other counties, the Peterson Companies responded, "Yes, but only if you can participate as Montgomery County did—by assembling the land, putting together a ground lease structure, building and operating public parking garages, and so forth."

Paseo Colorado, a mixed-use retail and residential project located adjacent to Old Pasadena, California, represents an evolution in thinking about downtown development, both by the city of Pasadena and by the development community. Both the old mall (Plaza Pasadena) and the new center (Paseo Colorado) were developed as public/private partnerships, with the city of Pasadena providing partial financing and other support. The three-square-block urban village replaces an earlier enclosed mall built as part of a 1970s redevelopment effort. In an attempt to revitalize Colorado Boulevard in the 1970s, the city pursued what was then a progressive idea: building a regional mall downtown. Through its redevelopment agency, the city acquired 14.9 acres (6.0 hectares) of land along Colorado Boulevard. Through the 1980s and 1990s, Old Pasadena came back to life through the efforts of building owners, developers, and substantial public investment in parking and other improvements. However, Plaza Pasadena concurrently began to decline, and the deadened streetscape along Colorado Boulevard increasingly became an impediment to the regeneration of the Civic Center area and the Playhouse District just to the east.

To address such issues, the city of Pasadena convened the Civic Center Task Force in 1997, which formulated the following objectives for the Plaza Pasadena site: (a) restore the city street grid, in particular the Garfield Avenue view corridor; (b) reintroduce retail activity to Colorado Boulevard; (c) provide for pedestrian circulation and gathering spaces; and (d) offer a mix of uses, including housing as well as retail. The emerging Paseo Colorado concept entailed the demolition of everything above the subterranean parking structure except the Macy's department store. TrizecHahn Development Corporation, which—through its forebear, the Hahn Company—had an ownership interest in Plaza Pasadena, participated in the Civic Center Task Force deliberations and subsequently chose Post Properties of Atlanta, Georgia, as a partner for the housing component of the project redevelopment.

As the project was structured, the city of Pasadena contributed $26 million in financing to the project, which was in the form of certificates of participation backed by the lease on the center's parking structures. Paseo Colorado today consists of 56 retail shops, a full-line Macy's department store, seven destination restaurants, six quick-service cafés, a health club, a day spa, a supermarket, a 14-screen cinema, and 387 residential units. Paseo Colorado has replaced the inward-looking mall previously built on the site with a project that reintroduces retail uses to street frontages, restores the urban block pattern and the axial view intended for the site, and provides for mixed uses and interior midblock retail space. The success of the project is spurring proposals for development of long-neglected vacant parcels adjacent to the site.

The city of Pasadena, California, provided partial financing for Paseo Colorado.

Ehrenkrantz, Eckstut & Kuhn Architects

Bayshore Town Center in Glendale, Wisconsin, was developed on a greyfield mall site.

Courtesy of Design Development Group

Retrofitting and Redevelopment of Car-Oriented Retail

Across North America, a generation of regional malls and strip centers is in decline. Although regional and superregional fortress malls in prime locations in affluent markets remain healthy, an increasing number of secondary and tertiary centers have gone dark. The trend is prevalent enough to have earned a term: greyfields. Factors attributed to a rise in greyfields include (a) department store consolidation, (b) a trend toward overretailing that renders as uncompetitive those centers with obsolete features and substandard tenant lineups, (c) the rise of online shopping, and (d) higher gasoline and energy prices that have strapped many consumers. Because of their desirable infill locations within largely built-out communities, many of the obsolete greyfield properties are increasingly being redeveloped as town centers or urban villages.

Examples of greyfield mall sites converted into town centers and urban villages are well documented: Bayshore Town Center in Glendale, Wisconsin; Mizner Park in Boca Raton, Florida; Winter Park Village in Winter Park, Florida; Paseo Colorado in Pasadena, California; and Mashpee Commons on Massachusetts's Cape Cod. The subject matter is large enough for a book of its own and was examined in the 2002 Congress for the New Urbanism publication, *Greyfields into Goldfields*.

18

The size of regional malls—including parking fields—represents a significant greyfield inventory of large parcels ripe for redevelopment. Infill sites that are in established markets, that are located on public transportation, and that have strong road connections are particularly attractive to developers. Many opportunities exist. Some estimate that there are 140 abandoned regional malls in America, and that in the coming years, more than 200 others are expected to be vacated.

A greyfield site can signify decline and disinvestment for a community. Additionally, such a site can represent a tremendous loss of potential tax revenue to a municipality. Accordingly, local governments are willing to get involved in the redevelopment of old malls and are likely to be willing to contribute financial assistance or another form of public assistance to a private developer.

A notable mall redevelopment is Winter Park Village, which is a 525,000-square-foot (48,800-square-meter), mixed-use lifestyle center located on the site of a failed regional shopping mall in Winter Park, Florida, an affluent older suburb of Orlando. The mall, which was built in the 1960s and was a traditional, inwardly focused center surrounded by surface parking, was successful for several decades, but it steadily lost tenants and customers during the 1980s and early 1990s as newer, more flashy malls opened nearby. Winter Park Mall's occupancy rate eventually fell to 30 percent. When a large-scale redevelopment plan that consisted of "essentially a souped-up strip center" was taken to the city of Winter Park for approval, municipal officials gave the proposal an icy reception. Donald Martin, the city's director of city planning, envisioned something different: a new urbanist, mixed-use project that would create a sense of place and transform the site into an urban village.

A revised, and ultimately approved, plan featured a pedestrian-scale streetscape with mostly two-story buildings aligned along a main street and with several secondary streets, many of which

Now a pedestrian-oriented, mixed-use destination, Clayton Lane in Denver, Colorado, is a redevelopment of a site that housed a Sears department store and auto center.

Courtesy of Frank Ooms Photography

tie into the city's existing street grid. The project's street system restores the street grid that had been in place before the 1950s, when planning for the original mall began. Street widths and lengths were kept narrow and short, and the roads were "jogged" in several places to slow traffic and to improve the pedestrian experience. Parallel parking along the streets adds to the project's urban feel, although most parking is located in large lots between buildings and at the development's edges. Private streets with sidewalks connect the interior of Winter Park Village with the surrounding area, making it possible for neighborhood residents to walk to the village. Today, the project features 350,000 square feet (32,500 square meters) of retail space including a 20-screen cinema, 115,000 square feet (10,700 square meters) of offices, and 52 loft apartments.

In addition to replacing obsolete enclosed malls, town center and urban villages can be developed as an intensification of land uses on an extant retail site. In the case of Clayton Lane in Colorado, a freestanding Sears department store and auto center with a 650-car parking lot located in Denver's Cherry Creek neighborhood was transformed into a 704,000-square-foot (65,400-square-meter), pedestrian-oriented, mixed-use redevelopment over four years. In 1996, Sears began exploring the possibility of redeveloping the site. Two years later, the company signed a lease with Whole Foods and started building the grocery store. However, the proposed designs for the remaining land were based on a suburban power-center model that retained the surface parking lots. The Cherry Creek neighborhood expressed a desire for a new urbanist plan with retail storefronts abutting the sidewalk and below-grade parking to help meet the neighborhood's need for more parking facilities.

Accordingly, Sears entered a joint venture with the Nichols Partnership. As of 2007, the 9.5-acre (3.8-hectare) project features a 170,000-square-foot (15,800-square-meter) corporate headquarters for the Janus Capital Group; a 196-room JW Marriott Hotel with a restaurant, a spa, a ballroom, meeting space, and an outdoor event courtyard; and 25 upscale condominiums. Totaling 336,100 square feet (31,200 square meters), the retail space includes a remodeled 133,000-square-foot (12,400-square-meter) Sears store with a new, detached, below-grade auto center; a Whole Foods market; and new shops and restaurants.

Development Flexibility

Long-term vision is the framework for a new development, and flexibility is a tool for implementing the vision; together, they provide the basis for plans at the outset, decisions during development, and adjustments at maturity. Without development flexibility, a town center or urban village will be unable to accommodate technological innovations, changes in the local community, and changes in retail and residential trends at large. Flexibility is necessary for long-term success.

Historically, town centers have grown and changed organically. Creating a new town center requires analogous flexibility over the course of development as markets shift, as consumer prefer-

Excelsior and Grand, located in a suburb of Minneapolis, Minnesota, was developed over four phases.

Courtesy of ESG Architects, Inc.

ences change, and as relationships among uses mature. Given the uncertainty of the future, a basic flexibility can be incorporated by designating mixed-use zoning that allows for density and use to shift within a project. Further flexibility can be ensured through phased development. Each completed phase is assessed for its success as a town center component, as well as its economic success. Even the efficacy of the street grid should be reviewed. Subsequent phases should be planned to respond to changes, to refine and build on successes, and to correct any weaknesses.

Phasing, while providing flexibility, should not be interpreted as a series of incomplete increments. The first phase should be a viable project in itself, which is able to thrive commercially and to establish the area as a growing town center. Each subsequent phase should merge with the existing environment to sustain viability and growth, thus enhancing the project and creating further opportunities.

Considerations of building design, block size, and infrastructure location also support future flexibility. Large floor plates and attention to fenestration may allow for adaptive use of buildings, thereby providing the basic requirements for retail, office, and residential uses. Large block sizes not only allow for the adaptable floor plates, but also allow for complete redevelopment into an entirely new use—should that change become appropriate in the future. Placing infrastructure around the outer edges of a surface parking lot so that later construction of a garage does not require reconfiguration also enables flexibility.

The components of flexibility are essential but must be approached in the context of a long-term vision. Adjustments in size, density, mix, and location of uses must maintain the integrity of the town center concept and must support the development of the community's core. Basic concepts such as the public realm, human scale, street grids, and overall quality cannot be compromised. The notion that a town center is built for the future—to endure beyond any of its current tenants and uses—is the vision that guides the development process.

Where parcels are developed over time by different developers or eventually are sold, this long-term vision is of paramount importance. It requires a master planner—a keeper of the flame—to maintain the integrity and quality of the plan over time. Where ownership is more diverse, the master planner may be the jurisdiction in which the town center is located, supported by a vocal community and property owners who are invested in the town center. The role of the community is particularly noteworthy because a successful town center is the true heart of the community. Its success depends on the community's continued relationship with the town center. Looking forward with both a long-term vision and flexibility is key to developing and sustaining a vibrant town center.

Incorporation of Existing Fabric

Where they exist, historic buildings should be included because they add value. The restored church at the heart of CityPlace in West Palm Beach, Florida, is a prime example (see case study on page 84). Iconic buildings can be elements in place making but are not essential. Buildings should reflect authenticity, genuineness, and honest design and should respect the local context. They can be eclectic, offer a variety of styles, provide for intimacy and serendipity, and present an element of surprise and possibly even grandeur. Architectural variety allows the town

DEVELOPMENT TRENDS

center to look as if it has been developed over time, which greatly contributes to the feeling of a place that is authentic.

Downtown Silver Spring (DSS) serves as another example where a historic site or building was renovated and incorporated into the new development. Among the underused structures that had fallen into disrepair was the historic 1938 art deco–style Silver Theatre and Silver Spring Shopping Center complex, a landmark of early 20th-century commercial architecture and one of the nation's first automobile-oriented shopping centers. The restored façade of the Silver Spring Shopping Center serves as a focal point of the new mixed-use complex. The center's limestone and granite façade has been returned to a close approximation of its original appearance; in fact, signage mirroring its historical counterpart has been put in place. The façade also features a re-created clock with art-deco numbering.

Montgomery County and the American Film Institute (AFI) signed a formal agreement to move the national arts organization's East Coast exhibition program from the Kennedy Center for the Performing Arts in Washington, D.C., to DSS, where it would occupy and operate the historic Silver Theatre. The county agreed to spend up to $7.8 million to restore the 400-seat theater and to develop an adjacent facility that would include a 200-seat theater and a 75-seat theater, as well as state-of-the-art audio-visual equipment, offices, a conference room and library, and concession and retail space.

Use of Storyboarding

Storyboarding is a way of telling a story about the imagined history of a town center or urban village. Traditional town centers evolved over the course of decades—if not centuries—and contrasting designs often developed through that organic growth. New projects lack the genuine patina of those town centers but seek to capture some of that richness. The design of the new projects is structured in a way that the buildings may seem to transition from older to newer, through varied architectural styles, even though they are built as part of the same project and possibly at the same time. The storyboarding and interpretation of a downtown that may have evolved over time are meant to enhance the experience of the town center, not to be read as an attempt at falsifying history or fooling visitors into thinking the project truly developed over several decades. The re-creation of past architectural styles can pay homage to the history of the region while it more closely connects the development to the local community.

Victoria Gardens in Rancho Cucamonga, California, is one example of a project where storyboarding was used (see case study on page 184). Four architecture firms—Field Paoli, Elkus Manfredi, Altoon + Porter, and KA Architecture—were hired to give buildings and streets different feels, as though various architects had designed them across time. Details such as sidewalk materials and plantings were varied. Certain buildings were even named after early settlers of the area. The result of those design choices is successful place making and the feel of a town center that grew with the region.

San Elijo Hills Town Center, which is north of San Diego, California, also achieved its architectural diversity through the use of varying building materials, as well as by varying the roof heights. The mixed-use town center project incorporates many different architectural themes to convey the sense that it has evolved over time. Intended to add to the visual vitality of the overall town center, architectural flourishes include the circular two-story design of the public library, the arched park entrance, the large central fountain in the town square, and a clock tower—all of which can be seen from the town square and contribute to the sense of place at San Elijo Hills.

Mizner Park in Boca Raton, Florida, draws its architectural inspiration from the regional Spanish Mediterranean design palette.

Cooper Carry

The Glen Town Center in Glenview, Illinois, uses storyboarding for the same purpose—achieving a look of having developed over time—but it actually has some historic buildings as part of the project (see case study on page 130). Hangar One, formerly an airplane hangar, was preserved in the design and now serves as part of the retail portion of the town center, as well as a focal point in the project. Some newer buildings were designed to complement the architecture of Hangar One, thus enhancing the experience of the project and honoring the history of the site as a former U.S. Naval Air Station. In this way, a story was created within the project while connecting to the local community through recognition of the importance of its naval history.

Using an imagined urban history can create heighten context sensitivity. Such projects are perceived as places that have qualities that are unique to them and their region. As an example, Mizner Park in Boca Raton, Florida, has an architecture that reflects the Spanish Mediterranean characteristics of the region, while Country Club Place has a different, specific expression that brought new design ideas to the Kansas City, Missouri, suburban context of the 1930s. As with the Glen Town Center, it is the uniqueness and specifically the character of the centers that makes them special and connects them to the community.

The Glen Town Center in Glenview, Illinois, uses storyboarding as part of its design but includes actual historical structures on the site.

Courtesy of OliverMcMillan

Design That Uses Dissonance

Skillful urban design is a necessity to avoid projects that are monolithic, dysfunctional, or otherwise unwelcome additions to a community's landscape. To avoid monotonous design, especially for larger projects and town centers, developers will sometimes require that several architecture firms be hired to design different parts of the project. Rather than the project's making architects adhere to strict design guidelines, some freedom in architectural expression will aid in the creation of interesting combinations of design. Jacoby Development, the master developer of Atlantic Station in Atlanta, understands this concept and required its residential developer partners to hire different designers and builders.

According to Susan Fainstein, the director of the urban planning program at Columbia University, "It is hard to create texture when everything is new, but [designers appreciate being] given these kinds of sites, like old steel mills. You can't develop them incrementally. You need a whole new address. It isn't a matter of momentum; you have to create a change in perception. And that requires a lot of capital and patient investors." (Lisa Chamberlain, "Building a City Within the City of Atlanta," *New York Times*, 24 May 2006.)

The Greene in Dayton, Ohio, purposefully uses varying design styles and building materials to create visual interest.

Steiner + Associates

Sometimes, buildings are intentionally designed to clash. In many of today's great cities, contemporary buildings sit next to historical ones; modern towers are built next to community relics from centuries ago. This juxtaposition of contrasting styles creates visual interest. The purposeful creation of these dissonant voices seeks to capture some of that allure.

With Bethesda Row in Maryland, Federal Realty hired three local architectural firms to collaborate with Cooper Carry on designs for the different phases of the project. The multiple ideas that were generated successfully hid the fact that the rather large buildings at Bethesda Row were all redeveloped at the same time. The individual retail tenants also were encouraged to design unique façades for their stores. For example, a skateboard shop has a stainless steel façade with bold lettering and lighting while a nearby upscale market has a storefront featuring an expanse of windows and soft-colored tiles. More than mere artifice, the attention to design has worked to create a successful urban environment.

One-story buildings, generally, do not effectively shape an attractive realm. Two-, three-, and four-story buildings are ideal because they are tall enough to define the space but not overwhelm

it. Taller buildings can work as well, although higher buildings will block sunlight, which can detract from the public realm. The larger the public realm spaces, the larger the buildings that can effectively surround them, such as with the skyscrapers near Central Park in New York.

The quality of materials and architecture visible from a public space shape and provide character to that space. Materials with lasting qualities and local appeal can establish authenticity; without such materials, the place may not be viewed as authentic or timeless. Buildings that face onto the signature public spaces must have a sense of permanence that makes a statement about the authenticity of the town center.

The scale of buildings at Del Mar Station in Pasadena, California, complements the public realm.

Photo by Jim Kumon

Civic Anchors

Libraries, theaters, museums, and recreation centers are among the civic anchors that can be incorporated into a design of a town center or urban village. Town squares can also serve as civic anchors when they provide a gathering place for cultural and civic events for the community. Civic anchors help to create an authentic town center.

In California, Victoria Gardens' Cultural Center incorporates a public library and a performing arts center in one. The 90,000-square-foot (8,400-square-meter) center also includes the 4,500-square-foot (420-square-meter) Celebration Hall building, where banquets and receptions are held. In Maryland, Rockville Town Square also used a library for a civic anchor. The 100,000-square-foot

(9,300-square-meter) library is located at the center of Town Square, and large bay windows on the ground story provide patrons with views of the development. In West Palm Beach, Florida, CityPlace includes the Harriet Himmel Gilman Theater for Cultural and Performing Arts, a central plaza, and assorted small urban spaces. Streets in the development can be closed for community events.

More Hotels and Offices

Increasingly, developers of town centers and urban villages are including hotels and office space in their projects. Clayton Lane in Denver, Colorado, incorporates both uses and partnered with the Denver-based Janus Capital Group to do so. Janus already had a reputation as a good corporate citizen—derived from sponsoring community events—and this reputation helped the developers win rezoning that included exemptions from a neighborhood height limit, which was a key factor in making the hotel and office components financially viable. The Class A Janus offices occupy 170,000 square feet (15,800 square meters) of space on seven floors. The 11-story JW Marriott

Hotel tower sits above 22,000 square feet (2,000 square meters) of retail space owned by Clayton Street Associates. Marriott leases the 5,200-square-foot (500-square-meter) courtyard located in the interior of the block next to the hotel restaurant.

Legacy Town Center in Plano, Texas, offers four types of hotels, all owned by Marriott: an economy-class extended-stay hotel, a hotel catering to business travelers, a larger hotel with meeting and conference facilities, and a luxury extended-stay hotel. In San Jose, California, the Hotel Valencia in Santana Row (see case study on page 158) is a boutique hotel that, like the shops around it, targets a high-end client base that is willing to pay a premium for luxury services. Town centers and urban villages should consider their target demographic of visitors when deciding which kind of hotel is best suited for the development.

Office activity in a town center can range from second-story office space above retail to a free-standing Class A high rise. An office market analysis evaluates existing office space in the region, including tenant types, building age, building size, and concentrations and occupancy rates, as well as planned developments, transportation improvements, and industry trends.

A children's library and cultural center provide a civic presence at Victoria Gardens in Rancho Cucamonga, California.

Photograph by Jennifer LeFurgy

The Hotel Valencia at Santana Row in San Jose, California, provides a place for visitors to stay overnight in the development.

Photograph by Jennifer LeFurgy

The Janus Capital Group World Headquarters is an office tenant at Clayton Lane in Denver, Colorado.

Frank Ooms Photography

As part of its mission to provide leadership in the responsible use of land and in creating and sustaining thriving communities worldwide, the Urban Land Institute (ULI) convened a smart growth workshop in 2006 to propose creative solutions for improving the quality of land use and development and to distill ten principles for developing successful town centers. During three days of intensive study, a team of planning and development experts drawn from around the United States toured and studied three very different town centers in northern Virginia: the Market Common, Clarendon in Arlington (see case study on page 140), Fairfax Corner in Fairfax, and Reston Town Center in Reston.

The ULI teams were made up of leading town center developers, public planners, architects, economic consultants, and property advisers. They visited the sites, reviewed information about the sites, and met as separate teams to set out their findings, conclusions, and recommendations. The teams then met jointly to debate, consolidate, and refine their conclusions. The lessons learned from the three town centers can be applied wherever the public and private sectors are wrestling with the challenges of creating sustainable town centers for their communities. The developments include those that are created from scratch on greenfield sites and those that are integrated with existing development by adding to or redeveloping those places, regardless of whether they are under single or multiple ownership. This section presents the results of ULI's workshop, which crafted ten principles for creating successful town centers and urban villages.

An aerial photograph shows Phase 1 of the Market Common, Clarendon, in Arlington, Virginia.

Courtesy of McCaffery Interests, Inc.

Ten Principles for Developing Successful Town Centers and Urban Villages

☐ CREATE AN ENDURING AND MEMORABLE PUBLIC REALM.

☐ RESPECT MARKET REALITIES.

☐ SHARE THE RISK; SHARE THE REWARD.

☐ PLAN FOR DEVELOPMENT AND FINANCIAL COMPLEXITY.

☐ INTEGRATE MULTIPLE USES.

☐ BALANCE FLEXIBILITY WITH A LONG-TERM VISION.

☐ CAPTURE THE BENEFITS THAT DENSITY OFFERS.

☐ CONNECT TO THE COMMUNITY.

☐ INVEST FOR SUSTAINABILITY.

☐ COMMIT TO INTENSIVE ON-SITE MANAGEMENT AND PROGRAMMING.

1. Create an Enduring and Memorable Public Realm

Developers, urban designers, and public officials increasingly view the public realm as the single most important element in establishing the character and marketability of a successful town center or urban village. Streets, plazas, walkways, civic buildings, and parking all play a part. A well-designed public realm functions as anchor, amenity, and defining element. The public realm is the connecting force between the residential, retail, office, and other components, thereby unifying the development as a whole.

CREATE A CENTRAL PLACE FOR THE COMMUNITY

A successful public realm is one in which commerce, social interaction, and leisure time activities mix easily in an attractive, pedestrian-friendly, outdoor setting. People are drawn by the simple enjoyment of being there. If that enjoyment is to be felt, the public realm and public spaces must be well designed and programmed.

A well-conceived public realm has the following attributes:

☐ **IT SERVES AS A COMPELLING CENTRAL SPACE** that people are attracted to for its placement, design, and surrounding uses. The space can be a street, a boulevard, a square, or a combination of all three with other urban design elements.

☐ **MOVEMENT BETWEEN USES IS EASY AND FLUID,** and sight lines facilitate wayfinding and encourage exploration.

☐ **EFFECTIVE PROGRAMS AND EVENTS ARE USED TO ANIMATE THE SPACE,** and the capacity of the management is sufficient to ensure successful programming for the space.

☐ **OPEN SPACES ARE SIZED AND SHAPED TO ALLOW EVENTS TO BE HELD IN THEM.** They provide stage areas and technical support where appropriate. They have appropriate lighting and landscaping that will allow people to feel safe in them.

☐ **THE PUBLIC REALM IS OPEN TO PROGRAMS** that are significant to the community, such as charity events, holiday events, and civic events. This programming allows the public areas to become true public places with lives and traditions of their own. Thus, the public realm becomes a part of the community that goes beyond simple commerce or public relations and ultimately becomes a place with a history. The public realm should allow for the integration of the people, the place, and the larger community.

☐ **THE PUBLIC REALM IS INCLUSIVE** and brings together all the different segments of the community that may wish to visit or use the public spaces.

☐ **AN EXPERIENCE IS CREATED AND DELIVERED** that the market values and that generates premiums for the residences and offices in the town center or urban village.

Festival Italiano is an annual celebration of Italian food, wine, history, and culture at Belmar in Lakewood, Colorado.

Photo by Diane Huntress

☐ **THE PUBLIC REALM IS INTEGRATED WITH ADJACENT USES** that significantly enliven the public space, such as bookstores, libraries, public buildings, cultural facilities, restaurants, and general retail. Each of those uses has its own vocabulary for meeting the street and interacting with the public space that must be carefully considered in the urban design plan.

☐ **BUSY AND FRAGMENTED CONTEMPORARY LIFE** is balanced with comfort and convenience—the public realm is a place that restores the soul.

☐ **HIGHLY VISIBLE AND EASILY ACCESSED,** the public realm is well connected to roads, public transit, and parking infrastructure.

☐ **WHETHER PUBLICLY OR PRIVATELY OWNED,** the public realm has a strong civic identity and feels like a public space. Freedom of speech and political expression, which are the hallmarks and traditions of historic town centers, are respected. The town center project, therefore, has a competitive edge over other conventional projects.

☐ **PUBLIC AND PRIVATE RESPONSIBILITIES ARE CLEARLY DEFINED.** For example, the streets might be public to the curb plus 8 feet (2.5 meters) of the sidewalk; the remaining ten feet (three meters) of the sidewalk might be private (where restaurants and stores can have a presence). Thus, the public sector has a role in day-to-day operations, but private expression and flexibility are allowed as well.

A plaza along Market Street at the Woodlands near Houston, Texas, provides a place for visitors to gather and for the community to hold events.

Ted Washington Photography

A grassy median divides the road into one-way loop routes at Birkdale Village in Huntersville, North Carolina.

Courtesy of Pappas Properties, LLC

Sidewalks were designed to be extra wide at South Campus Gateway in Columbus, Ohio, to comfortably accommodate large numbers of people and to encourage a pedestrian environment.

Photo by Brad Feinkopf

The big idea is to create a place that is *the place* to be—to make the place as authentic as possible, a place that will have lasting identity.

DEFINE THE PUBLIC REALM WITH STREETS, OPEN SPACE, AND PEOPLE PLACES

The key design elements for a town center or urban village are activity, walkability, good circulation, connectivity, and parking. A good plan has a street framework and a design that creates harmony among buildings and open space, the automobile and the pedestrian, work and leisure, and commercial and residential uses. It is critical to create a framework that elevates the pedestrian experience through great public spaces, good urban design, well-designed parking schemes, wayfinding strategies, and effective management plans.

A well-designed public realm includes several features:

☐ **A WELL-CONCEIVED STREET AND BLOCK PATTERN AND NETWORK:** A sound basic pattern and an effective street and open-space plan allow flexibility and adaptability that permit the public realm to evolve, change, and grow over time.

☐ **WELL-DEFINED AND ARRANGED STREETS,** sidewalks, plazas, squares, parks, promenades, courtyards, walkways connecting to parking facilities and surrounding areas, enclosed public spaces, public and civic buildings, cultural facilities, and parking facilities: These elements reinforce one another and work together to create gathering spaces and sidewalk areas where retail and leisure meet. The creation of compelling "outdoor rooms" and gathering places should be a highlight of the plan.

☐ **A HIERARCHY AND GUIDELINES FOR STREET SPACES AND USES,** including the width of streets and sidewalks, the heights of buildings, and the quality and level of landscape elements: Streets should be neither too wide nor too narrow, and this scaling will vary from street to street within the town center and with the scale and nature of the project.

☐ **SIDEWALKS THAT ARE SIZED ACCORDING TO THEIR INTENDED USE AND PLACE** in the overall scheme: Wide sidewalks are planned where restaurants and al fresco dining will be concentrated. Narrower sidewalks are planned on less intensively used streets. Pedestrian walkways from parking structures and surrounding areas are clearly linked to the signature space.

☐ **A SCALE THAT IS COMFORTABLE FOR PEDESTRIANS:** The buildings engage the street through fenestration, materials, awnings, and store signage and lighting. Storefront designs avoid banality and allow for differentiation, so each store can brand itself strongly. Pedestrian-scaled signage is big enough for drive-by traffic to see but is not obtrusively large.

☐ **ON-STREET PARKING THAT ANIMATES THE STREETS** with slow-moving vehicles, that provides a protective wall of cars for pedestrians, and that delivers convenient parking: Two-lane streets with two-way traffic and street parking on both sides work fine. Alternatively, central parks or narrow boulevards can be used to divide traffic into one-way loop routes on each side of the park or boulevard, with parking on one or both sides of each street, as was done at Mizner Park in Boca Raton, Florida; Market Common, Clarendon, in Arlington, Virginia; Birkdale Village in Huntersville, North Carolina (see case study on page 76); Southlake Town Square in Southlake, Texas; and Santana Row in San Jose, California.

An enduring, memorable public realm is characterized by a pleasant and walkable environment where pedestrians can window shop while at the same time others dine al fresco.

StreetSense

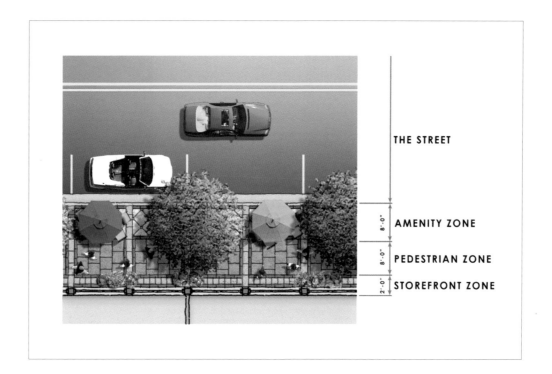

Native plantings in the courtyard at Del Mar Station in Pasadena, California, help create a public realm.

Photo by Conrado Lopez

☐ **LIGHTING THAT IS FOR PEOPLE, NOT CARS:** Storefront lighting is particularly effective in creating an attractive nighttime public realm, including both ground-level and upper-level windows and signage. Intense light is detrimental to an attractive atmosphere, and too little light makes the space seem unsafe.

☐ **LANDSCAPING AND ART THAT ARE ESSENTIAL INGREDIENTS IN PLACE MAKING:** Tree canopies are important defining elements in the public realm and provide shade in outdoor shopping environments. Water features, seating, landscaping features, street furniture, and signage all play important roles in defining the public realm. Public art creates unique places.

☐ **URBAN DESIGN THAT IS COORDINATED** so that the public realm emerges as each phase is built: For example, both sides of a street should be developed at the same time when possible, and signature public spaces should be surrounded by buildings as soon as possible. Public spaces without surrounding buildings and uses often look like vacant lots.

SHAPE AND SURROUND THE PUBLIC REALM WITH FINE BUILDINGS

A restored church sits at the heart of CityPlace in West Palm Beach, Florida.

Courtesy of Related Companies

Although the public realm is largely the space between buildings, that realm and space is very much affected and defined by the buildings that surround and shape the space. Thus, development of the designs for those buildings should involve careful consideration of the effect on the public realm. The buildings should be fine ones but should not necessarily have iconic architecture. Buildings and open space must be carefully integrated and mutually supportive, and the scale of buildings should complement the open space and avoid overwhelming it.

The quality of materials and architecture visible from a public space will shape and provide character to that space. Materials with lasting qualities and local appeal can establish authenticity; without such materials, the place may not be viewed as authentic or timeless. Buildings that face onto the signature public spaces must have a sense of permanence that makes a statement about the authenticity of the town center.

Historic buildings should be included where possible because they add value. The restored church at the heart of CityPlace in West Palm Beach, Florida, is a prime example. Iconic buildings can be elements in place making but are not essential. Buildings should reflect authenticity, genuineness, and honest design and should respect the local context. They can be eclectic, offer a variety of styles, provide for intimacy and serendipity, and provide an element of surprise and possibly even grandeur. Architectural variety allows the town center to look as if it has been developed over time, which greatly contributes to the feeling of a place that is authentic.

42

2. Respect Market Realities

A thriving town center or urban village is well tuned to the level and nature of the market that supports it. Understanding the market entails comprehending not only population counts and income levels, but also growth, competition, access, and aspirations. Each planned component should be evaluated separately to determine its basic strengths and the scope of its potential. But then all components must be evaluated together to determine their compatibility and the mix that works best for each component while offering an integrated, lasting environment. The goal is to provide a development that is greater than the sum of its parts.

In a mixed-use setting, retail uses drive residential and office uses. The retail component sets the tone of the general environment in two ways: through the tenant mix and through the nature of retail. First, the tenant mix makes a statement about the nature of the experience in the town center or urban village. Is entertainment offered through restaurants, bookstores, and cinemas? Performing arts or fine arts facilities also provide entertainment but generally do not keep people in the area if the retail components are not also present. Does the tenant mix include specialty stores? Are the tenants upscale, middle-of-the-road, or discount stores? Each provides different levels of browsing appeal, convenience, and customer traffic. Is there a supermarket? Supermarkets provide a convenience for nearby existing and future neighborhoods, and the type of supermarket—upscale or mainstream—is often one of the determinants of ambiance.

A Whole Foods Market serves as a neighborhood grocery store at 2200 in Seattle, Washington.

Courtesy of Vulcan, Inc.

Second, through the very nature of retail—trips to a variety of retail spaces by hundreds or thousands of customers per day, almost all on street level—a high level of pedestrian activity is sustained. Although office workers and residents generate additional pedestrian activity, they do not provide the ongoing volume of activity generated by the retail component. Further, proximity to stores and restaurants is a selling point for residential units and office space in town centers, whereas on-site residential and office activity is a small factor in most stores' locational decisions.

A retail market analysis answers two "big picture" questions:

☐ **WHAT TYPE OF RETAIL PROJECT CAN BE SUPPORTED BY THE MARKET?** Types include traditional neighborhood or community centers, more upscale centers commonly referred to as "lifestyle centers," power centers, regional and super regional centers, or hybrids consisting of elements of any or all of these. Hybrids are becoming increasingly common.

☐ **WHAT SIZE COULD THE RETAIL COMPONENT BE?** Size refers to built space and can range from less than 100,000 square 9,300 square meters) to more than 1 million square feet (93,000 square meters).

A retail market analysis follows six basic steps:

☐ **DETERMINE THE SPENDING PATTERNS OF THE SURROUNDING POPULATION**—where people shop, how much they spend.

☐ **DOCUMENT THE TYPE, SIZE, AND LOCATION** of existing and planned competitive retail facilities and districts, both nearby and in the region.

☐ **IDENTIFY THE LIKELY NEW TRADE AREA** on the basis of the analyses of those spending patterns and competing facilities.

Washingtonian Center in Gaithersburg, Maryland, was one of the first town centers to mix big-box discount stores with full-price and neighborhood convenience stores in a pedestrian environment.

☐ **CALCULATE TOTAL BUYING POWER IN THE TRADE AREA** and the amount expected to be captured by the new project.

☐ **TRANSLATE CAPTURED BUYING POWER** into supportable square footage.

☐ **CONDUCT A SITE AND TRAFFIC ANALYSIS** to ensure that the projected development can be accommodated.

Office space occupies ten floors at Mockingbird Station in Dallas, Texas.

Courtesy of RTKL Associates Inc.

Office activity in a town center or urban village can range from office towers to a single, second-level office space above a restaurant. Existing office space in the region, including tenant types, building age, building size, and concentrations and occupancy rates—as well as planned developments, transportation improvements, and industry trends—should all be examined when planning future office space.

Residential units in the development can include loft units, apartments over retail stores, apartment or condominium buildings, townhouses, and live/work units. Residential market analysis always looks at population growth projections and at market segments of the population that may be at a point in their life cycles where density and convenience are most attractive. Such segments include young professionals and empty nesters.

Higher-density housing is located around the town square at San Elijo Hills Town Center in San Marcos, California.

Photo by Sam Newberg

3. Share the Risk; Share the Reward

Developing well-designed, successful projects sometimes requires merging public and private interests and resources so that by sharing the risks, the rewards can also be shared. The conventional process of development is confrontational—an arm-wrestling contest between the local government and the developer to see which will get the best of the other from the process. Developing a collaborative partnership arrangement can avoid this zero-sum game and can produce outcomes that benefit all partners.

Public/private partnerships can be beneficial for a number of reasons:

☐ **LOCAL GOVERNMENTS CAN NO LONGER BEAR THE FULL BURDEN** of the costs for required public infrastructure and facilities. Private sector partners can share the costs.

☐ **NEITHER PRIVATE NOR PUBLIC INTERESTS ARE SERVED** by lengthy delays in the entitlement process. Public sector officials can facilitate the review and approval process.

☐ **PLANNING AND ZONING CONTROLS ARE OFTEN EITHER INADEQUATE** or too inflexible to ensure the desired public or private outcomes. The public and private sectors can work together to see that the process is less important than the desired outcome.

☐ **THE CITIZENS OF THE COMMUNITY MUST BE ENGAGED** and their views must be heard. Public and private partners can bring unique skills and resources to the process and together can nourish a supportive consensus within the community.

Today, public/private partnerships are seen as creative alliances formed between a government entity and private developers to achieve a common purpose. Other stakeholders, such as nonprofit

Crocker Park in Westlake, Ohio, is the result of a public/private partnership between Stark Enterprises and the city of Westlake.

Courtesy of Stark Enterprises

associations, have joined the partnerships. Citizens and neighborhood groups also have a stake in the process.

Although each such partnership is unique in its local implementation, most share development phases that are bounded by similar legal and political limits. In the first phase—conceptualization and initiation—stakeholders are surveyed for their opinions of the vision for the town center and the surrounding community, and the partners are identified. In the second phase, entities document the partnership and begin to define project elements, roles and responsibilities, risks and rewards, and decision-making and implementation processes. The partners negotiate the deal and reach agreement on all relevant terms. In the third phase, the partnership attempts to obtain support from all stakeholders, including civic groups, local government, and project team members. Project financing begins and tenant commitments are secured. In the fourth phase, the partnership begins construction, leasing and occupancy, and property and asset management. The process is repetitive and can continue beyond the final phase, when partners manage properties or initiate new projects.

A partnership is a process, not a product. Successful navigation through the process results in net benefits for all parties. The public sector can leverage and maximize public assets and can increase control over the development process to create a vibrant built environment. Private sector entities can receive more support throughout the development process and can have more certainty about approvals, timing, and acceptable and profitable outcomes.

A public/private partnership came together to develop Downtown Silver Spring in Silver Spring, Maryland, when previous attempts by private entities had been unsuccessful.

Photo by Julie Stern

RISKS

Public/private partnership projects can encounter various types of risk:

☐ **MARKET RISK:** Will the projected demand for space be realized?

☐ **CONSTRUCTION RISK:** Will the project meet the budget and the schedule?

☐ **OWNERSHIP RISK:** Will all the hazard of owning and operating a development, such as tenant leasing, be overcome?

☐ **INTEREST-RATE RISK:** Will the interest rate increase?

☐ **PERFORMANCE RISK:** Will the project achieve the public purpose for which the government justified its participation?

REWARDS

The most obvious rewards for the public are the net economic and fiscal benefits—jobs, infrastructure, taxes, fees, increases in the community's wealth and tax base—that can be produced by joint

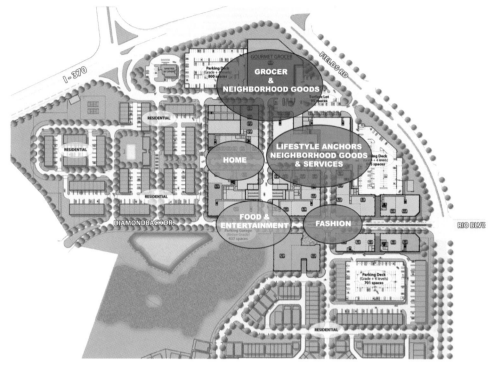

A merchandising plan considers the retail mix for target markets and the necessary balance of demographic and lifestyle groups.

StreetSense

The Soffer Organization worked with the Urban Redevelopment Authority of Pittsburgh to create SouthSide Works in Pittsburgh, Pennsylvania.

Courtesy of the Soffer Organization

action to overcome obstacles. Less tangible is the message that the community is on the move, that it is progressive in advancing the welfare of its residents. Public officials also enjoy gratification and recognition for their work. Meanwhile, the public benefits from a greater sense of identity, enhanced community amenities, and increased economic development.

The benefits to the private developer are perhaps the most obvious and readily measured, because a deal must be profitable after paying all costs associated with the investment of time and resources. In addition to the nonfinancial returns to ego and self-esteem that are produced by a

successful project, developers have reputations to build and protect if they are to participate in other deals and to continue to prosper.

Although the risks and rewards of a particular public/private partnership may be more easily measured in the private sector, the public concerns are no less important. A disciplined accounting of expected rewards and risks, or of benefits and costs, goes a long way toward demonstrating to key stakeholders and to the general public alike that a deal is worth doing. The public must know that all relevant factors of the deal are being considered—that risks are being carefully defined and evaluated and that steps are being taken to offset or mitigate the risks. Clearly, the objective of this accounting should be to show that the ultimate outcome of the partnership will be positive for both the public and the private partners as a result of their respective investments and risk taking. If an accounting of risks and rewards fails to show such a positive outcome, good reason exists to reconsider the undertaking.

4. Plan for Development and Financial Complexity

Financing and ownership issues in town centers and urban villages involve numerous levels of complexity beyond those that occur in most single-use projects. This complexity typically includes one or more of the following aspects:

☐ **LARGE OVERALL PROJECT SIZE** with large capital requirements;

☐ **A NUMBER OF USES THAT MAY BE FINANCED SEPARATELY** and have distinct financing requirements and market cycles;

☐ **PHASING STRATEGIES** that may require separate financing for each phase;

☐ **SEVERAL OWNERS OR EQUITY SOURCES OF CAPITAL,** including unusual ownership structures or multiple ownership structures;

☐ **MANAGEMENT ISSUES THAT AFFECT OWNERSHIP,** including covenants, maintenance and management agreements, condominium uses, and the like;

☐ **LENDERS WHO EVINCE A LACK OF UNDERSTANDING** or interest;

☐ **LONGER PREDEVELOPMENT PERIODS,** requiring high levels of upfront and at-risk equity;

☐ **LONGER CONSTRUCTION AND OVERALL DEVELOPMENT TIME FRAME,** thereby exposing the project to greater market and financial risk;

☐ **HIGHER OVERALL RISK,** requiring higher returns to compensate;

The scale of planned new town centers often requires phasing of development projects in line with market demand. Phasing may require different financing strategies because early phases are riskier, and later phases will be enhanced by the ongoing success and synergies of projects already completed.

StreetSense

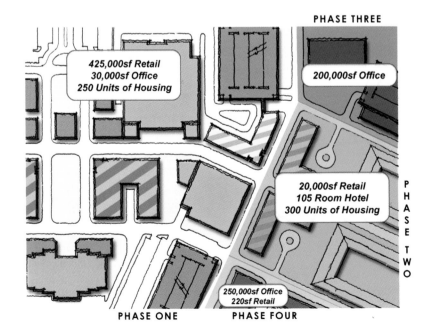

PHASE THREE

425,000sf Retail
30,000sf Office
250 Units of Housing

200,000sf Office

20,000sf Retail
105 Room Hotel
300 Units of Housing

250,000sf Office
220sf Retail

PHASE ONE   PHASE FOUR

PHASE TWO

PHASING PLAN

- RETAIL
- RESIDENTIAL
- MIXED-USE RESIDENTIAL OVER RETAIL
- OFFICE
- MIXED-USE OFFICE OVER RETAIL
- RESTAURANT
- MIXED-USE HOTEL OVER RETAIL
- CINEMA
- PARKING

☐ **HIGHER DEVELOPMENT COSTS PER SQUARE FOOT,** including higher legal costs, design fees, construction costs, and larger contingencies; and

☐ **PUBLIC FINANCING OPPORTUNITIES** and challenges.

USE A WELL-ORGANIZED, WELL-CAPITALIZED APPROACH WITH RESILIENCE AND VISION

To address issues of organization and capitalization, developers must be experienced, well organized, and very well capitalized. Town center and urban village developments are typically taken on by private developers that have a strong vision and the staying power to see developments through to completion. Developers must have a long-term outlook and must be ready to embark on a long process while staying with the project well into the operating period. They will need to develop a financial plan and structure that includes substantial upfront, at-risk equity to get the project through a long approval and predevelopment process—a process that may well end in a no-go decision, resulting in the loss of a lot of money.

Developers and their financial partners need to stay with the development well into the operating period because it may take some time to achieve the initial vision and to attain stabilized operations

The development of the Market Common, Clarendon in Arlington, Virginia, involved a complex arrangement and integration of different types of housing and retail uses.

Courtesy of McCaffery Interests, Inc.

and income, especially when phasing is involved. Profits on town centers are often made in the latter years of the holding period, when the project is fully built out and when performance is fully optimized. Success also requires implementing and fine-tuning an effective management plan. The management plan is essential to establishing solid operating performance over a period of years and to achieving the final vision. A long-term view and patient capital are essential ingredients.

Financial analysis must recognize the many ways in which mixed uses will affect construction costs, projected revenues, and operations. Although mixed uses will likely lead to higher revenues and greater profits, they also entail higher costs and greater risks. All those factors must be reflected in the financial planning process.

ATTRACT FINANCING AND WORK WITH MULTIPLE SOURCES

Financing for town centers and urban villages frequently involves equity from numerous equity capital sources, which may participate in the whole deal or just portions of it. Financing may involve multiple owners and equity sources for each element of the project. Legally defining where each ownership interest begins and ends is a unique and critical step in town center projects. Maintenance and management responsibilities for common area elements must be carefully spelled out in ownership and management agreements. Considerable time and effort must be spent on ownership and legal issues up front.

Significant time and effort will also be required to arrange and obtain debt financing. Multiple-use projects require lenders who recognize and understand what the various uses will be in the project, how they are operated, and how they fit and work together. The lender must be willing to finance something different, something that does not fall into standard single-use categories. This willingness is a difficult stretch for many lenders; thus the developer needs to spend time finding the right lender. Even then, a certain amount of time must be spent on educating the lender about the unique aspects of mixed-use development; public sector partners can often be helpful in this process.

Another approach is to arrange separate financing for each use, but this separation entails arranging numerous deals, which is in itself challenging. Finding a lender who understands the vision is important, and using multiple lenders may be necessary. Using multiple lenders can work for projects in which components are separately owned. For example, there could be different lenders for residential, retail, office, hotel, and other uses. Whatever lender approach is used, the plan must not be compromised to satisfy the lender.

CAPITALIZE ON PUBLIC FINANCING OPPORTUNITIES

Town center and urban village deals often involve public financing, which can provide much-needed funding but which comes with strings attached that may slow the process and increase its complexity. Municipal bonds and tax increment financing are often used to finance infrastructure improvements, parking garages, city halls or other public facilities, and other elements of a town center. Tax credits and many other public financing sources may be available. Putting together a solid public/private partnership can greatly enhance the viability and success of the project. It is important to look for ways to involve the public.

5. Integrate Multiple Uses

A mixture of uses is one of the most important qualities defining a town center or urban village. Historically, centers of towns or villages have contained a variety of uses that serve the broader community. The live/work/play concept was integral to those centers: uses such as markets, civic buildings, offices, hotels, and urban parks created a vibrant environment that was active during the day and the evening.

Developing a mixture of uses in a new town center or trying to introduce new uses to an existing center or urban area is not without challenges. Each use, although bringing potential benefits and synergies to the project, has different constraints and issues affecting its development. For instance, retail, residential, and office uses have different rates of absorption. Retail uses require a critical mass and prefer to open all at once. Residential and office uses, by contrast, have smaller and more defined rates of absorption and require longer time frames to develop. The inherent differences can hinder vertical integration, result in delay, and add cost to the development. A potential solution is to consider multiple uses instead of mixed uses.

Multiuse developments contain multiple uses; however, they are not completely integrated the way mixed-use developments are. In a multiuse scheme, for example, retail and residential uses are located within walking distance of one another but not within the same building. This development paradigm eliminates the complications that are often associated with the phasing and construction of traditional mixed-use projects. Multiuse development allows the entire critical mass of retail to be brought online at one time without having to be concerned with residential or office phasing.

Mixed uses are integrated vertically and horizontally. Multiuses are located within walking distance of each other and can be integrated horizontally, but the uses do not share buildings.

StreetSense

MIXED USE VS MULTI USE

Parking can either add value to or adversely affect a town center. Retail, residential, and office uses have similar demands for parking, whether they are in a single-use development or a mixed-use town center. Although a small amount of parking can be offset in a shared environment, the savings is not substantial, and large numbers of cars still must be accommodated for the commercial uses to be successful.

Phillips Place in Charlotte, North Carolina, has both mixed-use and multiuse components in a town center environment.

Lincoln Harris

Integrating parking in a town center requires consideration of the following key issues:

☐ **TYPICALLY, COMMERCIAL AND RETAIL PARKING** is more intensive than residential parking.

☐ **RETAIL AND OFFICE PATRONS PREFER LARGE FIELDS OF PARKING** that are public and open and that have great visibility.

☐ **RESIDENTIAL PATRONS PREFER SECURE, PRIVATE PARKING** arrangements that are located close to their units.

☐ **MUCH AS IN SINGLE-USE DEVELOPMENTS,** parking needs to be well distributed and balanced to meet parking needs throughout the development.

☐ **FACTORING IN THE REALITY AND SCALE OF PARKING DEMANDS** can make designing for an urban experience become difficult.

Retail and office patrons prefer parking that is public and open with great visibility. Residents prefer secure, private parking located close to their units.

StreetSense

First and foremost, town centers and urban villages are place-based developments. A sense of place functions as an anchor and helps distinguish the project from a typical single-use development. The integration of multiple uses with a multilayered system of streets, sidewalks, paths, alleys, and parks helps create a memorable environment for both the pedestrian and the patron arriving by car. Close attention must be paid to all those elements if the development is to be successful.

Integrating uses helps moderate the balance between vehicular traffic and pedestrian flow by creating different traffic peaks throughout the day and week. For example, residential uses help keep the retail uses and the sidewalks busy in the evenings, while office uses help generate activity in the project during the day. Having multiple uses or mixed uses is not as important as having a diverse range of uses.

DAYTIME PEDESTRIAN TRAFFIC FLOW

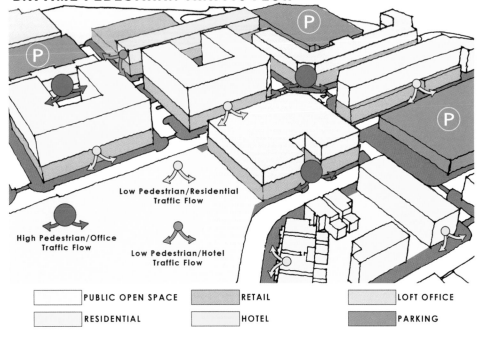

Low Pedestrian/Residential
Traffic Flow

High Pedestrian/Office
Traffic Flow

Low Pedestrian/Hotel
Traffic Flow

PUBLIC OPEN SPACE		RETAIL	LOFT OFFICE
RESIDENTIAL		HOTEL	PARKING

Residential uses help to keep the retail uses and sidewalks busy in the evenings while offices help generate activity in the center during the day.

StreetSense

EVENING PEDESTRIAN TRAFFIC FLOW

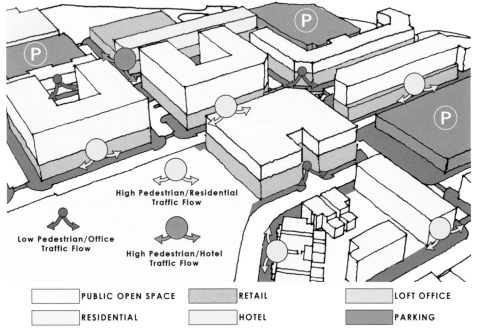

High Pedestrian/Residential
Traffic Flow

Low Pedestrian/Office
Traffic Flow

High Pedestrian/Hotel
Traffic Flow

PUBLIC OPEN SPACE		RETAIL	LOFT OFFICE
RESIDENTIAL		HOTEL	PARKING

Residential and office uses are two of the most critical uses for a town center or urban village because they accomplish the following:

☐ **CREATE SYNERGY WITH RETAIL USE,** including restaurants (a special subcategory of retail use).

☐ **ADD TO SIDEWALK AND STREET TRAFFIC**—retail loves crowds.

☐ **CONTRIBUTE—IN THE EYE OF THE USER**—to a more complete experience of a neighborhood environment.

☐ **COMPLEMENT AND FEED OTHER USES AND USERS,** for example, civic buildings and hospitality facilities.

Town centers and urban villages must be more than a brand name. They must connect with people at an emotional level and must be perceived by the community as belonging to it. The integration of multiple uses creates the diverse urban character that people identify with and enjoy. A mixed-use town development supports an environment that allows for a variety of activities, including working, living, shopping, entertainment, and leisure. The combination of residential, office, retail, and civic uses forms a neighborhood or district environment that will appeal to the public and be sustained by it.

Although integrating a mix of uses comes with complications in terms of cost, financing, phasing, and parking, the result can be a development with a perceived value that exceeds the sum of its parts. When executed properly, a town center or urban village is a lasting development that holds its value and becomes an enduring asset to a community.

6. Balance Flexibility with Long-Term Vision

Long-term vision is the framework, and flexibility is a tool for implementing a balance. Together, long-term vision and flexibility provide the basis for planning at the outset, for decisions during development, and for adjustments at maturity.

Historically, town centers and urban villages have grown and changed organically. Creating a new development requires analogous flexibility over the course of development as markets shift, consumer preferences change, and relationships among uses mature. Given the uncertainty of the future, a basic flexibility can be incorporated by designating mixed-use zoning that allows for density and for the use to shift within a project. Further flexibility can be ensured through phased development. Each completed phase is assessed for its success as a component, as well as its economic success. Even the efficacy of the street grid should be reviewed. Subsequent phases should be planned to respond to changes, to refine and build on successes, and to correct any weaknesses.

Phasing, while providing flexibility, should not be interpreted as a series of incomplete increments. The first phase should be a viable project in itself, one that is able to thrive commercially and establish the area as a growing development. Each subsequent phase should merge with the existing environment to sustain viability and growth.

Considerations of building design, block size, and infrastructure location also support future flexibility. Large floor plates and attention to fenestration may allow for adaptive use of buildings while providing the basic requirements for retail, office, and residential uses. Large block sizes not only allow for adaptable floor plates, but also allow for complete redevelopment into an entirely new use—should that become appropriate in the future. Placing infrastructure around the outer edges of a surface parking lot so that later construction of a garage does not require reconfiguration also enables flexibility.

The components of flexibility are essential but must be approached in the context of a long-term vision. Adjustments in size, density, mix, and location of uses must maintain the integrity of the

Victoria Gardens plans to continue to grow building by building and is using its parking fields as space for future structures.

RMA Architectural Photographers

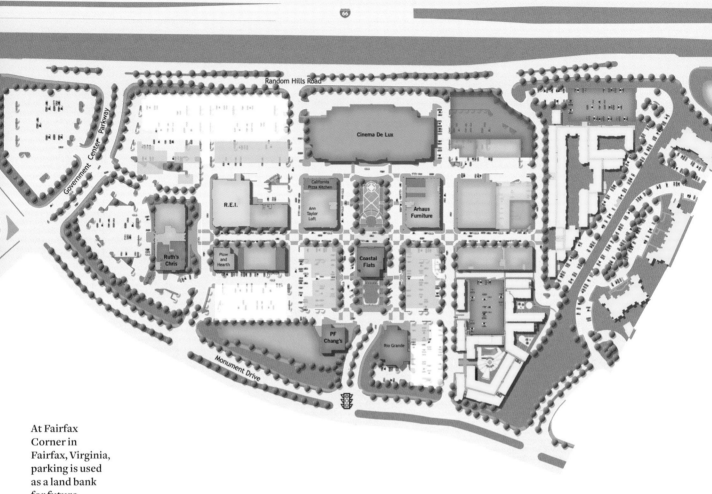

Random Hills Road

Cinema De Lux

R.E.I.

California
Pizza Kitchen

Ann
Taylor
Loft

Arhaus
Furniture

Ruth's
Chris

Plow
and
Hearth

Coastal
Flats

PF
Chang's

Rio Grande

Government Center Parkway

Monument Drive

At Fairfax Corner in Fairfax, Virginia, parking is used as a land bank for future higher-density development.

The Peterson Companies

development concept and must support the growth of the community's core. Basic concepts such as the public realm, human scale, street grids, and overall quality cannot be compromised. The notion that the project is built for the future—to endure beyond any of its current tenants and uses—is the vision that guides the development process.

Where parcels have been developed over time by different developers or eventually sold, that long-term vision is of paramount importance. It requires a master planner—a keeper of the flame— to maintain the integrity and quality of the plan over time. Where ownership is more diverse, the master planner may be the jurisdiction in which the town center or urban village is located, supported by a vocal community and property owners invested in the development. The role of the community is particularly noteworthy because a successful town center is the true heart of the community. Its success depends on the community's continued relationship with the town center. Looking forward with both a long-term vision and flexibility is key to developing and sustaining a vibrant town center.

7. Capture the Benefits That Density Offers

The development of an appealing, vibrant town center or urban village requires a well-designed mix of uses at a density high enough to achieve a critical mass of people on the street. A truly successful town center will be the most densely developed and lively part of the community.

Designing a dense town center requires the introduction of pedestrian-friendly spaces. In contrast to the automobile's domination of conventional low-density development, higher density makes the human scale possible. Imagine a densely developed, mixed-use center where people can easily walk along broad sidewalks lining attractive storefronts and can safely cross narrow streets as they move within the development. Now picture a conventional strip center set behind a large parking field and next to a wide highway. The former invites people to get out of their cars and stay with perhaps walking from shopping to dining and on to other activities. The latter dissipates the energy of the center by encouraging car-based "laser" shopping—park the car, buy the item, get back in the car, and leave.

Nonetheless, adequate and convenient parking is essential to the success of retail developments and is necessary for office and residential uses as well. Cars are the most important part of our transportation system, and people rely on their cars to get to stores, to get to work, and to get home. Accordingly, an efficient, well-designed parking system must be planned at the beginning.

At Easton Town Center in Columbus, Ohio, high density means more amenities, more liveliness, and more synergies between development components, plus more choices for the public.

Steiner + Associates

The Del Mar Station in Pasadena, California, is a transit-oriented development with a very high density and is located in a tradition-ally low-density community.

Photo by Warren Aerial Photography, Inc.

It is especially important that parking be shared among uses. Thus, parking that is used by office workers during the day can be used by residents or theatergoers at night. Well-managed, conve-nient, and visible parking facilities contribute greatly to a town center's appeal and incentive for use. It is important to remember, however, that one of the primary benefits of a dense town center is to keep automobiles in their place—supporting, not dominating. If cars and parking dominate the town center, the area will not achieve the overall livability and pedestrian friendliness that make the town center concept work.

The size of a town center and the amount of parking needed are based on the size of the target market. Is the town center appealing to a regional market, a community market, or perhaps just a neighborhood market? The bigger the market is, the higher the density threshold for the project. In any case, the goal is to build to the threshold of density that is necessary to attain a critical mass for that town center. For town centers that are already built, achieving this goal means reworking the master plan to allow for more dense development.

Higher density creates great places to live in six important ways:

☐ **HIGHER DENSITY HELPS CREATE** walkable neighborhoods.

☐ **HIGHER DENSITY SUPPORTS** housing choice and affordability.

☐ **HIGHER DENSITY HELPS EXPAND** transportation choices.

☐ **HIGHER DENSITY SUPPORTS** community fiscal health.

☐ **HIGHER DENSITY HELPS IMPROVE** security.

☐ **HIGHER DENSITY HELPS PROTECT** the environment.

Density increases opportunities for public transit and also for cross-shopping, thus keeping the whole center thriving by creating synergy among its various uses. In a development with shorter distances between the stores, restaurants, residential spaces, and offices, residents or office workers can easily become consumers. This kind of dense, mixed-use setting is very well suited to incorporating public transit access points, thus further increasing the appeal of the center and promoting walking.

Perhaps the most important fact is that denser development facilitates the creation of a sense of place. A place is full of energy if it is filled with people who have many places to go and things to do. What is a town center or an urban village without the liveliness that people bring to it? There is a direct correlation between that liveliness and high density. This fact makes high density a key element in achieving a town center development that feels authentic.

Density and transit are mutually supportive in urban village environments, such as with Mockingbird Station in Dallas, Texas.

Courtesy of RTKL Associates Inc.

63

8. Connect to the Community

One of the defining characteristics of town center and urban village developments is that they are very public and have strong connections with the surrounding community. The fact that patrons look on these places as public centers, not as managed shopping centers or private commercial developments, is an important distinction. Strong connections to surrounding neighborhoods, commercial areas, and park systems help reinforce the view that the development is accessible to all users. A sense of ownership and belonging separates and characterizes town centers from traditional shopping centers.

Connectivity requires an understanding of the complex interrelationships among planned uses, roads, pedestrian ways, transit, open space, and the surrounding neighborhoods.

StreetSense

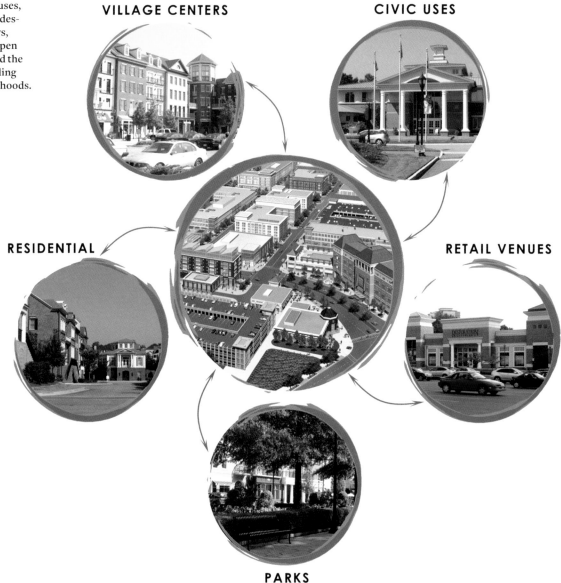

VILLAGE CENTERS

CIVIC USES

RESIDENTIAL

RETAIL VENUES

PARKS

Connectivity must include accessibility as shown at Victoria Gardens in Rancho Cucamonga, California.

RMA Architectural Photographers

Connectivity to a town center occurs at a variety of levels. The most obvious connection is through a well-designed series of roads at the arterial, collector, and local scales. Town centers, like other regional or semiregional destinations, can generate a high volume of vehicular traffic. Designing roads that are adequate to handle and distribute the traffic that feeds those centers is very similar to designing roads in conventional projects, until the roads diminish to a local capacity and the interface with pedestrian traffic intensifies. Town centers require an effective balance between pedestrian and vehicular traffic. Sidewalks, walkways, and bike trails are also key components that feed into and connect a town center to surrounding neighborhoods and other communities.

Town center and urban village developments typically have a retail and commercial component that is place based. High volumes of pedestrian traffic and a great sidewalk experience are critical to the success of such uses. The sidewalk environment should not be overlooked as an element that can fascinate and amuse pedestrians. Given enough width, sidewalks offer opportunities to accommodate small parks, fountains, cafés, and resting areas. Along with clear sight lines into the adjacent retail spaces, these components can make a sidewalk extremely effective in supporting a sense of place and expanding the experience of someone walking through the development.

Designing a great sidewalk requires consideration of five points:

☐ **SIDEWALKS NEED TO BE ACTIVATED** by being next to occupied retail space, residential stoops, and well-maintained lobbies for offices and other compatible uses.

☐ **SIDEWALKS NEED TO BE OCCUPIED,** with people always there throughout the day and evening.

☐ **SIDEWALKS NEED TO BE WELL MAINTAINED AND FREE OF LITTER.** Having an involved community presence is important in this respect.

☐ **SIDEWALKS NEED TO IMPART A SENSE OF PERMANENCE.** They should be lined by mature trees, high-quality landscaping, and high-quality materials.

☐ **SIDEWALKS NEED TO BE RETAIL-FRIENDLY,** safe, secure, and comfortable. These characteristics are achieved by making streets easy to cross (with on-street parking) and by providing inventive signage.

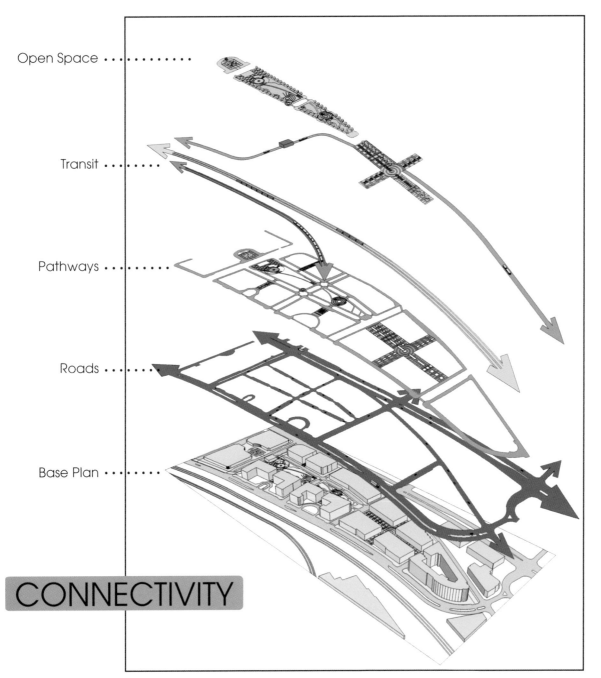

Open Space

Transit

Pathways

Roads

Base Plan

StreetSense

CONNECTIVITY

A multilayered approach to infrastructure and walkway systems needs to be considered. Although the car is still the primary mode of transportation to and from town center developments, public transit, bike paths, and trails can reach out to adjacent areas and can provide a natural means of access. The success of alternative modes depends on how well they can be integrated into the primary road system.

Open space can also be an important component linking a town center to a broader park system. This linkage is particularly the case with suburban town centers, where land areas and more generous open-space requirements create opportunities for connection to larger parks.

Apart from the physical aspects of connectivity, another very important type of connection occurs at the emotional level. Successful town centers have strong bonds of ownership with surrounding neighborhoods and communities. They are perceived as real places that have qualities that are unique to them and their region. As an example, Mizner Park in Boca Raton, Florida, has an architecture that reflects the Spanish Mediterranean characteristics of the region, while Country Club Plaza in Missouri has a different, specific expression that relates to the Kansas City suburban context of the 1930s. It is the uniqueness and specifically the character of those centers that makes them special and that connects them to the community.

Connectivity enhances transportation choices—driving, walking, and transit—and enhances the desirability and marketability of the town center at Broadway Plaza, Walnut Creek, California.

StreetSense

Another area that is often overlooked with respect to connectivity is the retail merchandising strategy. Regional content can apply to more than architecture or physical design. Some of the most successful town centers have a great number of local and national merchants. Good local tenants have roots in the community and are typically keyed into local trends and preferences. This connection is particularly true of restaurants and other food-related tenants, which have a strong sense of local tastes and put a lot of effort into creating places that are unique to their personalities.

Developing successful town centers is a very complicated process with many issues to consider. A system of roads and walkways that provide easy access to the center from the surrounding community is one of the most important elements to get right. Commercial uses, such as retail spaces, offices, and hotels, require high levels of traffic and visibility to thrive. Similarly, the place-based nature of a town center creates strong emotional connections with the surrounding community. A sense of uniqueness and specificity are characteristics that separate a town center from other developments or centers. Reinforcing connections at the physical and emotional levels strengthens the position of the center in the market and helps ensure its continued long-term viability.

9. Invest for Sustainability

Sustainability is not just a buzz word that stands for the use of green products and protection of the environment. Sustainable design uses a holistic approach that includes economic and social, as well as environmental, considerations. The goal of sustainable development is to be environmentally responsible and physically enduring while performing well over the long term. This kind of success requires adaptability and good economic and commercial performance. It also means having a strong and adaptable social fabric that makes people want to be in that place and return to it often.

One way to view the sustainability of any development is to observe (a) how enduring and memorable it is, (b) whether it is based on a long-term vision that is market based and flexible, (c) whether it is planned and financed for adaptability to its complex setting, and (d) whether it is well connected and well integrated with the surrounding community. Each of those characteristics is recognizable as reflecting some of the principles that are the subject of this book (principles 2. respect market reality; 4. plan for development and financial complexity; 6. balance flexibility with a long-term vision; and 8. connect to the community). They may each be examined in more detail in that context, but integrating all the principles wisely will achieve the framework for sustainability.

Good sustainable development of town centers often takes place on infill sites, but when it does occur in an outlying or greenfield setting, of special importance is that it be designed well. Infill sites reduce infrastructure costs, offer transportation alternatives, and restore or enhance local economic and social vitality. Regardless of the location, the project must be well connected to the surrounding environment (streets, parks, and trails) and to places where people can access public transit. Planning for sustainability means thinking beyond the car to incorporate other transportation choices such as walking, cycling, car-sharing, and using trains or buses. Public transportation that can facilitate independence at all stages of life and all income levels and that can provide easy access to quality-of-life amenities is important to every community.

An atrium within Clipper Mill in Baltimore, Maryland, features a green roof and the building's original trolley crane.

Patrick Ross Photography

For success over the long haul, investing in the public realm is as important as investing in store spaces, as demonstrated at Mizner Park in Boca Raton, Florida.

Cooper Carry

The enduring nature of sustainable development means that environmental considerations play an important role. The conventional practice in development is to engineer solutions to environmental problems: if it is too hot, more energy will cool it off; if it is too wet, a bigger pipe will carry the water away; if the landscaping is stressed, give it more water.

Before engineered solutions became the vogue, however, solutions to those issues existed—solutions that we seem to have forgotten in the interim. Among them were the following:

☐ **FACTOR THE LOCAL CLIMATE** into the design.

☐ **PLAN FOR WATER CONSERVATION** and recycling.

☐ **OPTIMIZE THE EFFICIENCY** of systems.

FACTOR LOCAL CLIMATE INTO THE DESIGN

Climate should be used as a design determinant. Climate is an important part of what makes a place unique. Vernacular building designs often reflect local climatic conditions. For example, in areas receiving a lot of snow, steeply sloped rooflines prevent a buildup of weight on the roofs. Designs should take advantage of building orientation, prevailing winds, and tree cover for cooling. The effect of the sun's rays should be managed to enhance or limit heating—covered arcades and building overhangs can shield visitors from the sun, rain, and snow. The albedo-temperature effect in cool-weather regions means that using dark colors on exterior surfaces will help warm the buildings and reduce energy costs; similarly, using light colors on exterior surfaces in warm-weather areas will reduce the need for cooling.

PLAN FOR WATER CONSERVATION AND RECYCLING

A variety of practices can be designed into a project to help conserve water. Water-conserving plumbing fixtures and faucets are some of the more obvious ones. Practices such as (a) using graywater and rooftop rainwater-harvesting systems to recycle water and (b) using natural drainage systems and pervious paving to recharge aquifers are becoming more common. Landscaping with native plants and drought-tolerant plants (xerescaping) that are adapted to the local climate and moisture conditions reduces the need for intensive irrigation.

OPTIMIZE THE EFFICIENCY OF SYSTEMS

Energy efficiency should be built into a project to minimize or eliminate the use of nonrenewable energy sources. The incorporation of passive solar and natural cooling principles enhances energy efficiency. High-efficiency heating, ventilating, and air conditioning systems—as well as lighting, appliance, and plumbing systems—will reduce energy consumption, diminish waste, and avoid pollution from the use of fossil fuels. The efficient use of lumber creates a tighter building envelope. The thoughtful integration of design, materials, and systems makes a project more comfortable, healthier, and potentially less expensive for owners and developers.

Other techniques can be used to prevent negative environmental impacts: (a) designing to reduce dependence on the automobile, (b) using resource-efficient materials, (c) reducing the quantity of materials used, (d) designing for durability and adaptability, (e) protecting local ecosystems, (f) conserving water, (g) ensuring the health of indoor environments, and (h) avoiding construction waste.

Sustainability requires having a flexible approach and thinking in the long term. Sustainability is the glue that binds financing, planning, zoning, designing, marketing, and building and that creates quality of life and a sense of community. Planning for sustainability does not stop at buildout. A strong, long-term strategy addresses the following:

☐ **CONTINUING PROGRAMMING** and amenities;

☐ **ENSURING CONTINUED ENVIRONMENTAL** responsibility;

☐ **SECURING A MIX** of uses;

☐ **MAINTAINING HIGH-QUALITY DESIGN,** particularly in architecture and programming;

☐ **UPHOLDING MAINTENANCE PLANS** (building, site, community, and infrastructure); and

☐ **FINANCING FOR LONG-TERM** management and care.

Another, perhaps simpler, way to view sustainable development is as high-quality development. A high-quality town center is sustainable when it promotes economic vitality, fosters environmental integrity, and encourages a lasting sense of community. Sustainable development promotes health, conserves energy and natural resources, is well connected to the community, and is economically successful.

At Kierland Commons, Scottsdale, Arizona, the high level of amenities, landscaping, and attention to every detail creates a memorable destination that people enjoy visiting and revisiting.

Design Workshop

10. Commit to Intensive On-Site Management and Programming

Town centers and urban villages are more than real estate developments. The project is designed to be the heart and soul of a community; as such, it functions as a public, as well as a private place. Residents and visitors to a town center are invited 24 hours a day, which means that management must be more intensive and ongoing than at a shopping center or other type of commercial development. Because a town center will be the densest, most diverse, and most active place in a community, management will likely be more complex and expensive, and it will definitely need to be more sophisticated.

Managing a town center or urban village is, in some ways, like operating a small city, and many of the functions that a local government performs in a real downtown must be performed by the private managers of the development. The scale of those functions will be proportional to the intensity and mix of uses and will need to be attuned to the needs of the different users. Operation and maintenance standards of the buildings and the public realm will need to be higher than in a city, as will security costs, because a town center competes directly with other nearby private developments, especially shopping centers. Potential conflicts must be understood in advance and avoided. For example, trash pickups must be arranged so as not to disturb residents or shoppers, and garbage rooms must be air conditioned so noxious smells do not waft through the tree-lined

streets or up to residents' windows. Management also includes such mundane but critical tasks as maintaining bathrooms that are spotless; fountains that work flawlessly; sidewalks and streets that are in top repair and litter free; flowers that are blooming, colorful, and healthy; and a tree canopy that is mature, trimmed, and healthy.

Management efforts, while intensive, should be unobtrusive, sensitive, and discreet. Too many security guards, too much overt control, and too many rules will make the center feel unnatural and uncomfortable. Management will need to be more politically astute than in a typical real estate development, because different segments of the public undoubtedly will take ownership of the center as strong community bonds are established and nurtured. This situation will require a constant interface with the public because it becomes, in essence, a partner in the ongoing operation of the town center.

Continuous programming of activities and events in the public spaces is a significant aspect of town center management. Such programming will ensure that visitors' experiences are memorable and pleasant. Management must remember that people who are at the town center are not just customers or consumers; they are also residents or other citizens who may not be there to buy anything at all but simply to experience community life. Planned events should include ongoing activities such as concerts and farmers markets, as well as community-defining events such as 4th of July fireworks displays. Unplanned events such as political rallies or community protests are also important because they deepen the center's connections to the community, but they need to be carefully coordinated with the day-to-day operations of the center to avoid needless conflict.

Marketing plays a role in ensuring a town center's long-term competitiveness and in ascertaining that significant opportunities exist for cross-marketing the center's various uses. Management should help coordinate such efforts to take advantage of the synergies they offer. A preferred customer card for residents is one example. A parking management program that includes valet parking, shared parking among the users of the town center, frequent monitoring of parking availability and conditions, and maintenance of high standards at parking entrances and in garages also helps market the center as a desirable and enjoyable place to come to.

The managers of a town center are its long-term champions, the keepers of the flame, and the ones who ensure continuity and who uphold standards as the center matures. Economic, social, and political conditions change, plus the managers' role, includes ensuring that the town center remains competitive in the broadest sense. This role is true whether the town center evolves under single or multiple ownership.

Managers carry out this role in numerous ways, first by leasing to the right mix of tenants and ensuring that the mix evolves as customer preferences and retail trends change. Second, they should ensure that all development adheres to the town center's master plan and vision as it matures. Third, they should draw up and enforce a set of covenants, conditions, and restrictions (CC&Rs) that clearly articulate the development standards and rules within the town center. The ideal master plan and accompanying CC&Rs should be drafted in ways that encourage flexibility, innovation, and change within a framework of high standards and compatibility with the founding vision of the town center.

At Mizner Park in Boca Raton, Florida, the public realm is open 24 hours a day, and the level of quality and attention to detail must be first-rate.

Cooper Carry

CASE STUDIES

Project	Location	Residential above Retail	Office	Hotel	Civic Anchor	Transit Linkage	Grocery Store	Public/Private Partnership	Suburban Infill	Urban Infill	Master-Planned Community
Birkdale Village	Huntersville, North Carolina	■	■				■				■
CityPlace	West Palm Beach, Florida	■	■		■	■	■	■		■	
Crocker Park	Westlake, Ohio	■	■			■	■		■		
Downtown Silver Spring	Silver Spring, Maryland			■	■	■	■	■		■	
East 29th Avenue Town Center	Denver, Colorado	■	■		■	■	■			■	■
Excelsior and Grand	St. Louis Park, Minnesota	■				■	■	■	■		
The Glen Town Center	Glenview, Illinois	■				■			■	■	■
The Market Common, Clarendon	Arlington, Virginia	■	■			■	■			■	
River Ranch Town Center	Lafayette, Louisiana	■	■	■	■	■	■		■		■
Santana Row	San Jose, California	■		■	■	■			■		
South Campus Gateway	Columbus, Ohio	■	■				■	■		■	
SouthSide Works	Pittsburgh, Pennsylvania	■	■		■	■			■	■	
Victoria Gardens	Rancho Cucamonga, California		■		■	■		■			■
Zona Rosa	Kansas City, Missouri	■	■								

 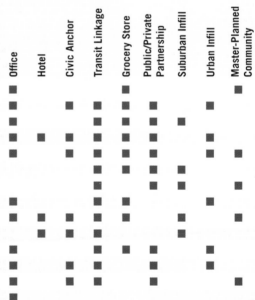

Birkdale Village

HUNTERSVILLE, NORTH CAROLINA

As is common in many parts of the United States, national retail chains and master-planned communities are changing the complexion of formerly rural areas. Northern Mecklenburg County in North Carolina was such a place, but the citizens decided that they would have a voice in how they grew. The town of Huntersville chose to confront its rapid growth head on by adopting a zoning ordinance to encourage compact development instead of automobile-dependent uses.

Pappas Properties, LLC, and Crosland, Inc., developed Birkdale Village, which is a mixed-use town center and the first project to meet Huntersville's new zoning requirements. The center combines 233,000 square feet (22,000 square meters) of street-level retail shops and 54,000 square feet (5,000 square meters) of office space with 372 apartment units and a 16-screen, 53,000-square-foot (4,900-square-meter) movie theater that surrounds a town green where residents and visitors gather for community events.

Birkdale Village's use of residential units over street-level retail stores helps create the vibrancy of an urban village.

Courtesy of Pappas Properties, LLC

Background

Huntersville is located about 15 miles north of Charlotte and is in Mecklenburg County. The town is one of the fastest-growing communities in North Carolina. Hunterville's population increased from 1,300 in 1980 to 25,000 in 2000, and as of early in 2008, the town's population had climbed to an estimated 40,000. Huntersville, along with the towns of Cornelius and Davidson, make up the area known as "North Meck." Many residents commute to downtown Charlotte using Interstate 77 by car or express bus service. Nearby Lake Norman, built to create power for the region, is a recreational attraction that now encompasses a sensitive wetland on the edge of the Huntersville.

In 1994, local residents who were concerned about the area's rapid development approached the mayor and the town council. The residents were concerned that the rural charm and small-town feel that made Huntersville an attractive community would be lost forever. Council members issued a one-year moratorium on development. However, they did not want to permanently deter new construction, so they compromised by organizing a visioning process that would encourage sensible development that is appropriate to Huntersville's scale.

In 1996, the Huntersville town commissioners approved a new, mandatory zoning code based on the collaborative visioning process. The code promotes new construction in the town's urbanized areas and along the town's existing and proposed transportation corridors, while preserving open space. It also applies new urbanist principles in "Traditional Neighborhood Districts" that include an emphasis on public spaces, street and building design, and connectivity for pedestrians.

Birkdale Village was the first large-scale, mixed-use development to be approved under the new zoning code. The property is bounded by an office park on the east and by the Greens at Birkdale, which is a new urbanist residential community on the north. The area also includes two golf course communities and a regional shopping center. To ensure connectivity and easy access to the center from the surrounding area, the site plan includes a grid street system that is flanked by sidewalks and includes a pedestrian path and a bridge that link Birkdale Village to the office park and the Greens at

Birkdale Village. Completed in 2002, the development is a 52-acre (21-hectare) pedestrian-oriented and mixed-use project that defied the area's status quo development patterns.

Drawing on the Past

In 1997, Pappas Properties acquired the site from Forest City enterprises and soon partnered with Crosland Inc. Pappas Properties is perhaps best known for the development of Phillips Place, which is considered one of the nation's first "lifestyle developments" and is located in Southpark near downtown Charlotte. Pappas Properties also brought its previous experience of working with the town of Huntersville on the approval of Birkdale, which is a golf course community. For Crosland, Birkdale Village was a continuation of the innovative, high-quality development for which the company historically has been recognized. The firm applied its 66-year history of managing construction and developing residential, office, and commercial projects to help create a seamless, welcoming home for residents and a shopping and entertainment destination for visitors.

In designing this project, which was patterned on New England coastal towns, the developers aimed to integrate and minimize conflicts between uses so they could create a place where people would enjoy living, shopping, and socializing. Because 81 percent of the residential units are located above retail stores, the developers paid special attention to parking, directional signage, lighting, noise, and street access while considering the needs of all users. The two- to four-story buildings have high-pitched roofs and are faced with a combination of brick, Hardiplank fiber cement siding, and cedar shakes.

Birkdale Village's main street is built on a traditional street grid system at a pedestrian scale with parking at the rear of the buildings. On-street parking is also available in parallel and angled space. A linear park runs the length of the main street, and a village green is located at the center of the development. The open space acts as a divider to slow traffic and also provides a connection between the pedestrian and built environments, while the village green serves as a point for community gathering and as a setting for many outdoor activities and events. The grid-street pattern links Birkdale Village to the surrounding neighborhood, which includes 491 single-family homes and townhouses. The residences, which are part of the Greens at Birkdale Village, were developed at the same time as the village center.

The developers of Birkdale Village have facilitated continuous foot traffic on the main street by clustering retail and entertainment uses along this corridor. The clusters roughly correspond to where the three cross streets intersect the main street to form blocks that are approximately 400 feet (120 meters) in length. At the central green, patrons find marquee restaurants and retail offerings. From this area, restaurant patrons may chose to walk either to the east, where they find the entertainment cluster that includes the movie theaters and the small retail shops, or to the west, where they can shop in the fashion and home furnishing stores on the west end of the green.

Clustering uses such as restaurants and stores around the central green facilitates foot traffic along the main street corridor and helps reinforce the sense of community.

Courtesy of Pappas Properties, LLC

Birkdale Village also includes junior anchor retailers such as Dick's Sporting Goods and Barnes & Noble Booksellers. To help maintain the pedestrian orientation of the main street, these retailers are located one block south of the main street, where pedestrians experience maximum exposure to automobile traffic on Sam Furr Road while they also remain within walking distance of the main street stores.

To better accommodate pedestrians' needs, the design team considered how pedestrians would move through the village. The team considered where the pedestrians would park, where they would stop to rest, where they would unload their packages, and how they would interact with other pedestrians. The distance between parking, sidewalks, crosswalks, public gathering spaces, and outdoor furniture was minimized to provide a pleasant street experience. The manageable 400-foot (120-meter) block length allows pedestrians to move between shops without being overwhelmed by the building scale. Additional curb cuts were added to the sidewalks to provide an easier transition from the street to the sidewalk for pedestrians with disabilities and for those pushing strollers.

The synergy created from the interaction of the residential, entertainment, and retail uses is most evident in the evenings, when activity is in full swing at the restaurants and stores and when

Open spaces with benches, landscaping, and a centrally located fountain at the village green contribute to the pedestrian-friendly environment.

Courtesy of Pappas Properties, LLC

residents are home from work. The location of residential units that are above the retail space adds to the bustling environment. Residents use their main street residential access to become a part of the street activity, thus venturing out to visit the restaurants, shops, and cinema and to walk their dogs. During the evenings, the residents can be seen sitting on their balconies while they watch the street activity.

Birkdale Village was modeled on New England villages and uses architecture that includes high-pitched roofs and bright white wood accents.

Courtesy of Pappas Properties, LLC

Old Charm, Modern Retail

The residents of Huntersville wanted to keep the area's small-town character intact, and the developer's achieved this goal through the project's density and architecture. However, the importance of bringing national retailers to Birkdale Village should not be understated. Although their involvement resulted in the higher costs that are associated with more tenant improvements, it also reassured lenders that the project would succeed.

Retailers such as Banana Republic, Victoria's Secret, and the Gap, which traditionally locate mostly in regional malls, provide an added amenity for residents, as well as attract shoppers from a wider market area. Although 40 percent of the national retail tenants occupy 65 percent of the gross leasing area, Crosland, which is responsible for retail tenant recruiting and for leasing, continues to work to attract local retailers so Birkdale Village can maintain a unique product mix that includes restaurants, gift and specialty shops, clothing and jewelry stores, and service retailers such as a copy center and a hair salon. The influence of the high-caliber national retailers has attracted top-quality local businesses to Birkdale Village without the need to offer rent subsidies to local retailers.

Huntersville residents have responded positively to Birkdale Village and have seen it as a realization of their plans to curb sprawling, low-density development. In May 2003, Pappas Properties and Crosland recaptured their investment, receiving more than a 20 percent premium when they sold their majority interest in Birkdale Village to Inland Retail Real Estate Trust Inc., which is based in Northbrook, Illinois, and is now known as Developers Diversified Realty.

Birkdale Village

HUNTERSVILLE, NORTH CAROLINA

www.birkdalevillage.net

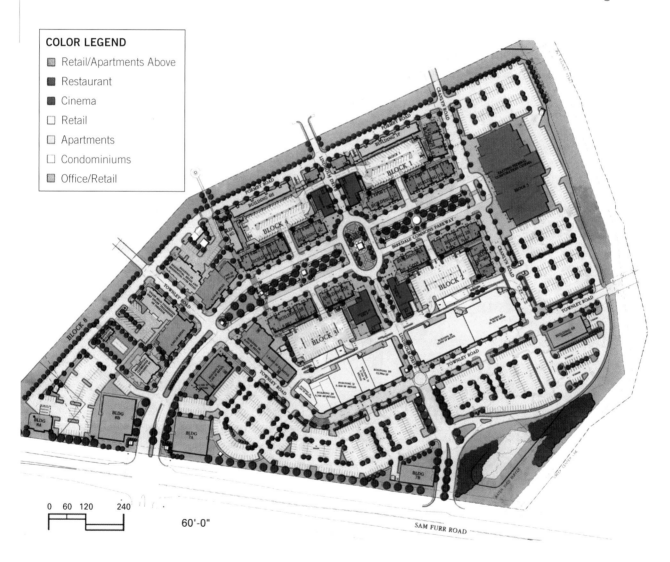

COLOR LEGEND

- ■ Retail/Apartments Above
- ■ Restaurant
- ■ Cinema
- □ Retail
- □ Apartments
- □ Condominiums
- ■ Office/Retail

0 60 120 240

60'-0"

Site plan.

Courtesy of Pappas Properties, LLC

PROJECT TYPE

Town Center in a Master-Planned Community
Single Owner

Site Area:	52 acres/21 hectares

LAND USE

Use	Square Feet	Number of Establishments/Units
Office:	54,000	
Retail:	233,000	57
Entertainment:	53,000	
Residential (rental):		372
Parking:	15,500	
Transit Linkages:		None

DEVELOPMENT COSTS

Site Acquisition Cost:	$7,000,000
Site Improvement Cost:	$11,700,000
Soft Costs:	$8,800,000
Construction Costs:	$55,000,000
Total Town Center Development Cost:	$82,500,000

DEVELOPMENT SCHEDULE

Planning Began:	1997
Ground Breaking:	2000
Phase I Complete:	September 2001
Phase II Complete:	2003
Town Center/Urban Village Buildout:	2003

DEVELOPMENT TEAM

Developers:

Crosland, Inc.
Charlotte, North Carolina
www.crosland.com

Pappas Properties, LLC
Charlotte, North Carolina
www.pappaspropertiesllc.com

Owner:

Developers Diversified Realty
Beachwood, Ohio
www.ddr.com

Master Planner:

Shook Kelley
Charlotte, North Carolina
www.shookkelley.com

Architect:

The Housing Studio
Charlotte, North Carolina

Landscape Architect:

Land Design
Charlotte, North Carolina
www.landdesign.com

CityPlace

WEST PALM BEACH, FLORIDA

CityPlace revitalized downtown West Palm Beach, Florida,
and stands as a testament to the power of public/private partnerships. The development, which is
designed with a Mediterranean theme, includes national retailers, local specialty shops, restaurants, residential units, a cultural center, a 20-screen movie theater that is inspired by the Paris
Opera House, and a $3.5 million "show" fountain in the central plaza. Opened in 2000, CityPlace
has spurred millions of dollars of development in surrounding areas, including a convention center,
and it has helped draw residents back to West Palm Beach's downtown. The developers are now
planning additional office and residential uses.

One of the key players in CityPlace's success was then-mayor Nancy Graham, who worked with
the development team to create an innovative and successful deal. Graham was West Palm Beach's
first elected "strong mayor" in 1991. One of her priorities was to revitalize the downtown area,
which had slid into decline and was pocked with vacant buildings. In 1993, while attending a
Mayor's Institute on City Design, Graham was inspired by the revitalization efforts of Mayor Joseph
Riley of Charleston, South Carolina, and by his use of a sensitive, compact urban design. Upon
returning to West Palm Beach, however, Graham discovered that her city's zoning and regulatory
codes would have to be overhauled. She appointed a new staff and commissioners who were
receptive to change and who began to plan innovative ways to acquire land and to demolish vacant
properties.

Graham soon revitalized parts of West Palm Beach and improved public amenities, but more
than ten contiguous blocks in the central downtown still remained vacant. Developer Henry Rolf
had quietly assembled the parcels during the 1980s, but his enterprise collapsed with the real
estate markets at the end of the decade. The city lacked both the funds needed to acquire the site
and the development expertise needed to carry out the type of urban, mixed-use development that
the mayor envisioned. Graham convinced the city to accept some financial risk by borrowing $20
million from Florida's Sunshine Fund to acquire the site and to support $55 million in bonds to be
repaid though tax increment financing. The city then issued a request for proposals (RFP) and

selected a team that would become CityPlace Partners. To speed along the process, the city took on all of the permitting work for the project. From the time that the bid was awarded to ground breaking took only 18 months.

Commercial Activity

CityPlace contains an assortment of shops, restaurants, and entertainment. Macy's provides a 110,000-square-foot (10,000-square-meter) anchor and has agreed to create a slightly smaller new urban concept store for the project. The retail also includes a 20-screen Muvico Parisian cinema with bar service, a Pottery Barn with residential uses above it, and a 23,000-square-foot (2,000-square-meter) Publix grocery store. CityPlace Partners attracted high-profile restaurants, including Legal Seafood, Mark's City Place, and Ruth's Chris Steak House.

In addition to CityPlace's retail and entertainment mix is a new office building, CityPlace Tower. The $110 million, 18-story office project is the first office building to be built in West Palm Beach

CityPlace was the product of a public/private partnership among the city, Related Companies, and Crocker Partners.

Courtesy of Related Companies

since 1989 and was conceived by the original CityPlace designers Elkus/Manfredi Architects. CityPlace Tower includes hurricane-resistant construction and redundant power source capability through emergency generators, through multiple high-speed connections to the Internet "backbone," and through multiple telecommunications providers for uninterrupted power and for access to vital computer files. The 300,000-square-foot (28,000-square-meter) building will complement CityPlace's European-influenced architecture and will feature pedestrian-friendly elements that will be linked to CityPlace shops and housing. The project is scheduled for occupancy by the first quarter of 2008.

Housing Choices

CityPlace offers a diverse assortment of rental and for-sale housing units. At the time of its development, some people commented that housing was an unproven use and an unnecessary risk for town center projects. However, the CityPlace team viewed housing as a means of generating round-the-clock street life, which was central to the project's long-term success.

The current housing mix includes 51 private townhouses, 33 garden apartments, 128 luxury rental apartments in high-rise buildings, 264 mid-rise rental apartments in three building, and 38 rental flats along with 56 live/work lofts that are located above storefronts. Much of the higher density housing is located in apartment buildings of the main street and envelopes the large parking garages that are located within the interiors of two blocks.

The new CityPlace South Tower, which is slated for completion in 2008, is a 20-story, 420-unit project. The project will include touch-screen monitors that will allow residents to order their car to

CityPlace has inspired development in the nearby Clematis Street district, which connects to CityPlace through a free trolley system.

Courtesy of Related Companies

be brought around and to make dinner and spa appointments. One-, two-, and three-bedroom residences will range in size from 800 to 1,600 square feet (75 to 150 square meters) and will be priced from $300,000 to more than $1 million.

Mediterranean-Inspired Design

The mixed-use core of the site is centered around a plaza and consists of four large blocks that are further broken up by alleyways and side streets. The pattern of streets and blocks in CityPlace provides multiple connections to nearby downtown neighborhoods, such as the recently restored Clematis Street district.

A former First United Methodist Church sits in the middle of the main plaza and forms the heart of CityPlace. Built in 1926, the church was one of the largest Spanish Colonial Revival structures of its day. It has been carefully restored and adapted as an 11,000-square-foot (1,000-square-meter) hall that is used for cultural performances, community events, and art

CityPlace's design creates highly textured streetscapes with buildings of varying scale.

Courtesy of Related Companies

exhibits. The church also serves as a visual anchor that lends the project a sense of history and authenticity.

The streets of CityPlace are lined with parallel parking spaces, plus varieties of street trees, large potted plants, and climbing trellises that are covered with flowering vines. Sidewalks range from six to ten feet (two to three meters) in width at key intersections and are buffered by bollards and lampposts that help to narrow the distance that the pedestrians must walk while crossing an intersection. The sidewalks are composed of tile mosaics; the streets, at certain intersections, are paved with bricks to heighten drivers' awareness that they are in a pedestrian zone.

Parking is provided in four large decks that are located in the back of the multistory buildings on either side of the main street, Rosemary Avenue. In the northern half of the site, the parking decks are concealed in the interiors of blocks and are accessible by means of a service alley. Parking decks to the south abut a commuter rail line that stops at a nearby station. The decks are connected to buildings, streets, and plazas through use of attractive pedestrian passageways.

CityPlace's architectural details play off a southern Mediterranean theme and feature exposed rafters, canvas awnings, tile and metal rooftops, and wrought iron and wooden balconies on the upper floors where residential units overlook the street life below.

To emphasize public gathering spaces, several outdoor dining areas surround the main plaza, and the landscaping includes benches, shady plants and trees. The project also includes a foun-

Plazas with fountains and wide sidewalks composed of tile mosaics, which are buffered from vehicular traffic by bollards and parallel parking spaces, help create a pedestrian environment.

Courtesy of Related Companies

tain that is a piece of civic art by day and that provides shows of water, light, and fog choreographed to music by night. Smaller plazas, courtyards, and fountains are located on both the first and second levels of the project, and the streets can be closed for festivals and events.

Performance

Since opening in 2000, CityPlace has survived the ups and downs of Florida's real estate markets. Several retailers have turned over, but vacancy rates remain low. Fifty-one townhouses, which were part of the original residential component, sold out in just ten days. CityPlace Partners, a joint venture that is managed by the Related Companies, remains optimistic about the new residential and office components that are now under development.

CityPlace enjoys both the coordinated marketing and management of a regional shopping mall and the municipality's support in programming community festivals and events. The project is having a positive effect on adjacent properties, such as the Clematis Street district and the Palm Beach County Convention Center that opened in 2003. (CityPlace Partners had planned to build the convention center hotel, but the deal with the city fell through.) To protect the city's prior redevelopment effort in the Clematis Street district, the downtown development authority and the developer have funded a free trolley system that connects the district with CityPlace in a continuous loop for seven days a week, 12 hours a day.

CityPlace has achieved a synergy with surrounding uses that will continue to benefit its long-term performance, because it is located in a "cultural triangle" defined by the nearby Kravis Center for the Performing Arts, the Dryfoos School of the Arts, and the Norton Museum of Arts.

Upper-level residential units feature balconies with wrought iron railings, thus helping connect residents to the activity on the street.

Courtesy of Related Companies

CityPlace

WEST PALM BEACH, FLORIDA

www.cityplace.com

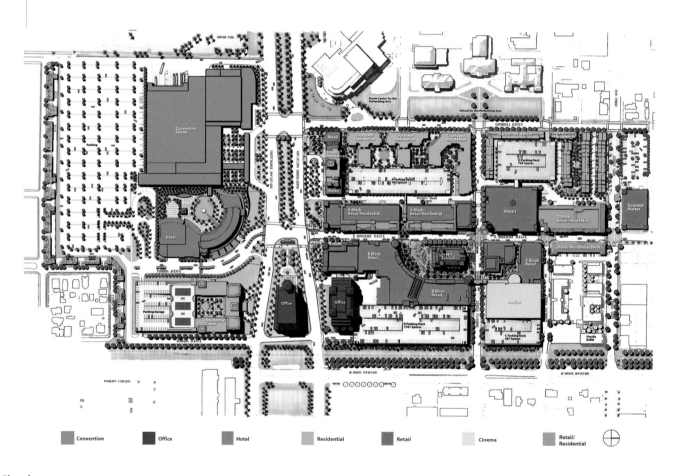

Site plan.

Courtesy of Related Companies

PROJECT TYPE

Town Center on a Redevelopment Site
Single Owner
Site Area: 72.9 acres/29.5 hectares

LAND USE

Use	Square Feet	Number of Establishments/Units
Office:	750,000	
Retail:	600,000	80
Residential (rental and condo):		900
Parking:		3,300

CIVIC/CULTURAL/OTHER

Harriet Himmel Gilman Theater for Cultural and Performing Arts, a central plaza, and assorted small urban spaces

Transit Linkages: Regional Rail, Bus

DEVELOPMENT COSTS

Site Acquisition Cost:	$20,000,000
Site Improvement Cost:	$55,000,000
Total Town Center Development Cost:	$217,000,000

DEVELOPMENT SCHEDULE

Planning Began:	1996
Ground Breaking:	1998
Town Center/Urban Village Buildout:	2008

DEVELOPMENT TEAM

Developers:

Related Companies
New York, New York
www.related.com

Crocker Partners
Boca Raton, Florida
www.crockerpartners.com

Owners:

CityPlace Partners
New York, New York

Related Companies
New York, New York
www.related.com

Palladium Company
New York, New York

O'Connor Capital Partners
New York, New York
www.oconnorcp.com

The Related Group
Miami, Florida
www.relatedgroup.com

State Teachers Retirement System of Ohio
Columbus, Ohio
www.strsoh.org

The City of West Palm Beach
West Palm Beach, Florida
www.cityofwpb.com

Master Planner:

Elkus Manfredi Architects Ltd
Boston, Massachusetts
http://www.elkus-manfredi.com/

Master Planner (Cultural Arts Center):

Rick Gonzalez, REG Architects
West Palm Beach, Florida
www.regarch.com

Landscape Architect:

Bradshaw Gill & Associates
Ft. Lauderdale, Florida

Public Partner:

City of West Palm Beach, Florida

Crocker Park

Crocker Park, which was developed through a public/private partnership between Stark Enterprises and the city of Westlake, Ohio, is a mixed-use center located 15 miles west of downtown Cleveland.

Scott Pease

Located in Westlake, which is a second-ring, affluent Ohio suburb that is approximately 15 miles west of downtown Cleveland, Crocker Park is a town center that has been developed on one of the city's few remaining commercial parcels. With 1.7 million square feet (158,000 square meters) of retail shops, restaurants, a movie theater, residential for-sale and rental units, and office space that are located in a pedestrian-friendly environment, Crocker Park has branded itself as a major suburban destination.

During the 1990s, the city of Westlake sought to develop the vacant 75-acre (30.4-hectare) site by using a town center concept. Although studies showed the retail development was underserved, the city resisted the notion that it should become "just another mall." Stark Enterprises and the landowner approached the city with a proposal for a mixed-use development. A citywide referendum was required to allow mixed-use development on the site, which voters approved in 2000, and Phase I of Crocker Park opened in 2004.

Public/Private Partnership

Crocker Park is a public/private partnership between Stark Enterprises and the city of Westlake. The city worked with the developer to allow appropriate zoning for the project to move forward, and it provided public financing of a portion of street improvements.

The approvals process for Crocker Park was complicated and lengthy. Although the planning staff and the city council generally agreed on the concept of a mixed-use development, the city of Westlake's zoning code was "ultra-Euclidian" and did not allow a mixed-use development, even for planned unit developments. As a result, the city required a referendum in 2000 to approve a zoning change on the site to allow for a mix of uses. The referendum was controversial and opposed by some community residents and by some owners of retail centers in the area who mainly cited increased competition. However, in 2000, the referendum was ultimately passed, which allowed Crocker Park to move ahead.

For the city to ensure that Crocker Park is a balanced, mixed-use community and not "just another mall," its development agreement with Stark Enterprises is very specific. The agreement

stipulates that no more than 35 percent of all space in each phase of development is retail and that more than 50 percent of all space in each phase of development must be residential. This restriction applies to all phases of Crocker Park, and it has been adhered to in Phase I. Future phases will include additional retail and housing, and possibly other uses, such as a medical facility and a hotel.

On-street parking is provided in Crocker Park, but it is metered. The city of Westlake did not have any metered parking before Crocker Park, so it had to create a system to enforce violations. Under the agreement, Stark Enterprises and its on-site security provider issue tickets to the violators, and the city enforces both follow-up and payment of tickets.

An Inviting Design

Designed by Street-Works and inspired by Mizner Park and Santana Row, the general concept of Crocker Park is a mix of uses that are located in a pedestrian-friendly street system. The various uses throughout Crocker Park are unified by similar building heights, massing, materials, and a well-designed and attractive streetscape that helps to create a sense of place for the entire development. The architecture is borrowed from a variety of styles and is intended to appear as if it has been built over time.

All streets at Crocker Park are new. The two major streets include a boulevard (Crocker Park Boulevard) with a wide center median and a main shopping street (Main Street) that crosses it. The intersection of those two streets features a roundabout. The median on Crocker Park Boulevard contains food stands, kiosks, a fountain, an oversized chess set, numerous benches, and other public space for gathering, plus a restaurant that was added in 2007.

Crocker Park includes 1.7 million square feet (158,000 square meters) of space, with 610,000 square feet (57,000 square meters) of retail space and restaurants, 225,000 square feet (21,000 square meters) of office, 160 apartment units, and more than 400 for-sale townhouses and condominiums. A 16-screen theater was expanded from an existing 11-screen facility that was part of an existing retail center immediately to the north. The older retail center, called Promenade, is also owned and managed by Stark Enterprises. Promenade has been integrated into the design and operation of Crocker Park. Crocker Park is approximately two-thirds complete.

The apartment units are located in three-story buildings above retail space along Main Street to the south of Crocker Park Drive. Those units include a variety of one- to three-bedroom unit designs,

With more than 1.7 million square feet (158,000 square meters) of developed space, Crocker Park features housing over retail, as well as office space over retail.

Scott Pease

94

with corridors that connect directly to parking structures behind the buildings. Most, but not all, of the stores in such mixed-use buildings contain clothing-related tenants, which achieves two goals: (a) it concentrates similar retail types on the site, thus creating synergy, and (b) it mostly avoids having restaurant and entertainment tenants in mixed-use residential buildings, which limits the residents' complaints about noise and smells.

To maintain continuity of building massing, the three-story mixed-use retail and apartment buildings south of the roundabout at Crocker Park Boulevard are matched by two-story retail uses on the north, with all four corner buildings having similar height. Barnes & Noble and H & M are the two tenants that have two-story stores.

Anchor tenants and larger restaurants are in more prominent locations, such as corners or terminating vistas at the end of streets. Barnes & Noble, H & M, Abercrombie & Fitch, Z Gallerie, Gap, Banana Republic, Cheesecake Factory, and Claddagh Irish Pub are all examples of corner retail spaces, and the Regal 16 movie theater and Dick's Sporting Goods are terminating vistas. Trader Joe's is another anchor tenant located in an accessible and prominent standalone building on the south end of the site. There is a significant presence of local and regional retailers, although the majority are national chains.

Design guidelines were created to control the appearance of everything at Crocker Park—from street and sidewalk widths to signage and building materials. The guidelines emphasize the pedestrian scale and a sense of place. A variety of building materials give the appearance that the project

Human-scaled architecture— and parallel parking spaces to serve as a buffer between the sidewalks and the street— creates a pedestrian-friendly zone.

Courtesy of Stark Enterprises

has been built over time. Guidelines for Crocker Park Boulevard, for example, dictate 14-foot (four-meter) -wide drive lanes, nine-foot (three-meter) -wide parking lanes, 18-foot (five-meter) sidewalk widths, a minimum of 35 percent of sidewalk paved with brick, tree spacing of 30 feet (nine meters) and caliper of six to eight inches (15 to 20 centimeters), and a street light every 60 feet (18 meters).

The pedestrian environment is held in high regard. Sidewalks are extensively landscaped with numerous trees, benches, and planters that are aligned with the curb edge, and a row of on-street parallel parking further separates the pedestrians from moving traffic. Padded couches and chairs are even provided so visitors can sit—although only in warmer months. Many of the pedestrian crosswalks are raised, and a different paving material such as brick is used to differentiate and to alert drivers to slow down.

Meridian Park entices visitors to relax and play a game of chess or to rest on the benches while enjoying the landscaping.

Courtesy of Stark Enterprises

Wayfinding is addressed by numerous kiosk maps that are located throughout Crocker Park. A visitor and information desk is located on the Crocker Park Boulevard median that faces the roundabout.

The city required that 50 percent of all parking be located in structures rather than in surface lots. There are four parking structures— each one predominantly hidden—with easy access to, but not necessarily visible from, the main pedestrian streets. Many of the surface parking lots are located behind buildings or are temporary in lieu of additional development.

The Crocker Park development, which accommodates pedestrian and automobile traffic, as well as public transit, connects to a nearby arterial road through its grid-patterned streets.

Courtesy of Stark Enterprises

The western end of the site is the more residential section, with a number of for-sale housing types developed by the Coral Company, which is a partner developer and local builder of upscale housing. The various products that are offered include a mix of townhouses and condominiums. One new concept that has been introduced at Crocker Park is called "liner lofts." Those units are townhouses that wrap, or line, larger structures, thus reducing the number of blank walls and façades.

The for-sale housing at Crocker Park features styles that are new to Westlake, especially considering the residences' location in the town center. They maintain the design themes of Crocker Park, with a variety of building materials and an emphasis on walkability, as the residential streets also contain sidewalks that easily link to the rest of the site. The rental and for-sale housing together provide a range of housing options for young professionals and empty nesters in a town center setting that is not found elsewhere in suburban Cleveland.

An Approach to Market the Crocker Park Brand

Crocker Park has established itself as a branded location in the area. The town center acts as a place to live, shop, work, eat, and gather. As a result of the combined uses that are being well integrated by a unified design, the whole is in some ways greater than the sum of its parts, and its various uses perform better than their competition in the marketplace. For example, whereas other rental housing in Westlake offers concessions, units at Crocker Park are full even though rents are higher to begin with.

Stark Enterprises manages Crocker Park and focuses on the branding of the whole development. Most stores share common hours, and various events are organized throughout the year, including a July 4th celebration with fireworks, a fine art festival, a farmer's market every Saturday in warmer months, and a Christmas tree–lighting ceremony that takes place on the Saturday before Thanksgiving each year.

Many of the management and maintenance aspects that most visitors don't see include daily sweeping of streets, clearing sidewalks with leaf blowers, watering plants, covering and uncovering outdoor cushioned chairs and couches, and even replacing pieces of the oversized chess set. It is such meticulous attention to detail that keeps the town center inviting to residents and visitors alike.

With its elegant design and pedestrian environment, combined with its mix of uses that are positioned well to complement one another, Crocker Park has succeeded in becoming a true town center.

Bay windows in the residential units above ground-floor retail connect people to the activity on the street level.

Courtesy of Stark Enterprises

Crocker Park

WESTLAKE, OHIO
www.crockerpark.com

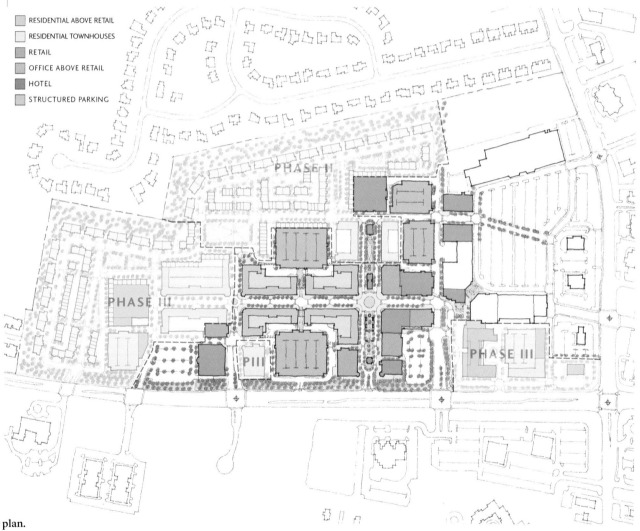

RESIDENTIAL ABOVE RETAIL
RESIDENTIAL TOWNHOUSES
RETAIL
OFFICE ABOVE RETAIL
HOTEL
STRUCTURED PARKING

PHASE I

PHASE II

PHASE III

PHASE III

PIII

Site plan.

*Courtesy of Stark
Enterprises*

PROJECT TYPE

Town Center on a Vacant Site
Separate Owners
Site Area: 75 acres/30.4 hectares

LAND USE

Use	Number of Square Feet	Establishments/Units
Office:	225,000	
Retail:	610,000	
Residential (rental, condo, primary residence):		368
Parking:		3,039 (584 surface and 2,394 structured)
Transit Linkages:		Bus

DEVELOPMENT SCHEDULE

Planning Began: 2000
Ground Breaking: 2003
Phase I Complete: October 2004
Additional Phases: TBD

DEVELOPMENT TEAM

Developers/Owners (Mixed-Use Core):
Robert L. Stark Enterprises
Cleveland, Ohio
www.starkenterprises.com

Carney Group
Cleveland, Ohio

Developer/Owner (Single-Family Perimeter Housing):
The Coral Company
Cleveland, Ohio
www.thecoralcompany.com

Master Planners:
Street-Works
Alexandria, Virginia

Bialosky + Partners
Cleveland, Ohio
www.bialosky.com

Architects:
Bialosky + Partners
Cleveland, Ohio
www.bialosky.com

Richard Levitz
Shaker Heights, Ohio

Meleca Architecture
Columbus, Ohio
www.melecaarchitecture.com

Communication Arts, Inc.
Boulder, Colorado
www.commartsdesign.com

Landscape Architects:
MSI Design
Columbus, Ohio
www.msidesign.com

Hank Rapport
Cleveland, Ohio
www.starkenterprises.com

Engineers:
Korda/Nemeth Engineering, Inc. (MEP)
Columbus, Ohio
www.korda.com

McNamara/Salvia, Inc. (Structural)
Boston, Massachusetts
www.mcsal.com

Thorson Baker and Associates, Inc. (SMEP)
Richfield, Ohio
www.thorsonbaker.com

Neff & Associates (Civil)
Parma Heights, Ohio
www.neff-assoc.com

Horton Lees Brogden Lighting Design (Lighting)
New York, New York
www.hlblighting.com

Environmental Graphic Designers:
Communication Arts, Inc.
Boulder, Colorado
www.commartsdesign.com

Maestri Design
Seattle, Washington
www.maestridesign.com

Market Researcher:
Stark Enterprises
Cleveland, Ohio
www.starkenterprises.com

Public Partner:
City of Westlake
Westlake, Ohio
www.cityofwestlake.org

Downtown Silver Spring

SILVER SPRING, MARYLAND

Downtown Silver Spring (DSS) is an urban, mixed-use infill and rehabilitation project that is anchored by restaurants, stores, offices, public spaces, and cinemas in Silver Spring, Maryland. The town is an inner-ring suburb of Washington, D.C., that had experienced decades of flight and changing demographics. After several unsuccessful attempts to redevelop downtown Silver Spring, a public/private development partnership came together to create a gathering place for this urban community: a live/work/play environment featuring a traditional urban street format that integrates existing structures and new construction. The project, which has spurred further redevelopment in the area, features approximately 440,000 square feet (41,000 square meters) of retail space, 185,000 square feet (17,000 square meters) of offices, a 179-room hotel, 23 movie screens in two facilities, more than 3,800 parking spaces, and public plazas and other open space.

DSS has been developed by a public/private partnership that is governed by a development agreement between Montgomery County, Maryland, and the private sector developer, PFA Silver Spring, LC. PFA represents a partnership among the Peterson Companies, Foulger-Pratt, and Argo Investment Company, which are all Washington, D.C., metropolitan area–based firms with broad experience in developing office, retail, residential, and mixed-use projects. The agreement called for $189 million of private investment for the retail, office, residential, and hotel components. The county initially agreed to provide $132 million for the acquisition of land; for the demolition of existing structures; for building two public parking garages; for streetscaping, a live performance theater, and a civic building; and for the restoration of the historic 1938 Silver Theatre and the façade of the Silver Spring Shopping Center.

Planning and Design

The entire project was designed to be compatible with the existing art deco architecture and to be considerate of the scale of the neighborhood. The restored façade of the historic art deco Silver Spring Shopping Center serves as a focal point of the new mixed-use complex. The shopping cen-

Downtown Silver Spring (DSS) is a mixed-use, urban infill, and historic rehabilitation development in Silver Spring, Maryland, near Washington, D.C.

Courtesy of the Peterson Companies

ter's limestone and granite façade has been returned to a close approximation of its original appearance. Where signage for a People's Drug Store once spelled out "DRUGS" in chrome art deco letters above the entrance, similar lettering now spells out "BREAD" above the Panera Bread restaurant and bakery. On the opposite corner, a "RADIO" sign has been replaced by "MY EYE DR." (The new signs were conceived—and paid for—by the retail tenants.) The façade also features a re-created clock with art deco numbering.

A second-floor addition was set back from the original structure to minimize its visual impact, and a multicolored, illuminated "DOWNTOWN SILVER SPRING" sign is located between the two halves of the upper addition. In front of the center and its small parking area (which, as the area's first free, storefront parking lot, is as historically significant as the shopping center itself) sits an elliptical landscaped park that is faced by a five-foot-high (1.5-meter-high) stone wall that has metal letters that spell "SILVER SPRING." A sheet of water falls across the face of the wall and behind the letters, pre-

DSS was developed by a public/private partnership governed by a development agreement among Montgomery County, Maryland, and the private sector developer PFA Silver Spring, LC, which is a partnership among the Peterson Companies, Foulger-Prattt, and Argo Investment Company.

Courtesy of the Peterson Companies

senting a visual and an aural reminder of the community's namesake. Walkways connect the historic shopping center with new development and public gathering places.

The second focal point of DSS is the new Silver Plaza, an internal public courtyard that includes a fountain, a neon sculpture, some seating areas, and additional lighting for performances and other public events. During warm weather, the fountain transforms the center of the courtyard into an array of water plumes emanating from a colorful 26-foot-diameter (7.9-meter-diameter) mosaic of glass tiles. The same tiles and designs appear on an adjacent stairway that leads to the upper level of the plaza, where several restaurants and a Gymboree facility are located. The 35-foot-high (10.7-meter-high) neon sculpture wraps around the elevator tower behind the fountain. Designed to draw people into the project, the plaza opens onto and includes Ellsworth Drive, which runs through the center of DSS and can be closed to automobile traffic, creating a pedestrian mall between Georgia Avenue and Fenton Street.

The project was able to use much of the existing road grid, minimizing the need for new infrastructure. Large tracts along the edges of the site were formerly used for county parking structures and are now used for public parking. The importance of the public parking component cannot be understated; the county-owned parking structures are fully integrated into the development, linking visitors directly to retail, entertainment, office, hotel, and civic buildings by breezeways, walkways, bridges, and other connections. With more than 3,800 spaces, the parking structures provide ample, convenient, and inexpensive or free parking for project users. (Parking costs $0.50 an hour on weekdays and—as a result of PFA's agreement to pay the county $125,000 per year for ten years—is free on weekends and evenings.)

DSS has breathed new life into the adjacent City Place multilevel urban mall. Although not part of DSS, City Place falls within the project footprint; particularly at the street level, no clear boundaries exist between City Place and DSS. PFA relocated the City Place loading dock to create continuous retail space along Ellsworth Drive.

Entertainment

PFA originally planned to commence construction on a multiplex movie theater in fall 2001. But attracting a mainstream cinema chain to anchor the entertainment portion of DSS proved to be an elusive goal. A fully negotiated lease with Edwards Cinema failed when the company went bankrupt in mid-2000. Many other theater chains started scaling back their expansion plans in early 2001, and another signed lease—this time with Muvico—fell through after the company was unable to secure financing. In mid-2001, the development team decided to rearrange its phasing schedule, speeding up the project's plans for a restaurant/retail area dubbed "restaurant row."

The development team worked closely with neighborhood leaders to design DSS for the local community. As a result, among the shops in the project are a hardware store, a Whole Foods Market, a video store, a wine shop, a dry cleaners, an interior design shop, a blinds store, and a photo shop.

Courtesy of the Peterson Companies

Silver Spring is one of three county-designated urban districts that provide the area with extra county services and facilities. Montgomery County envisioned DSS as a catalyst project that would revitalize its core and spur further redevelopment.

Courtesy of the Peterson Companies

Although the cinema complex initially was seen as necessary to attract restaurant tenants, PFA was able to negotiate contracts with five restaurants and three specialty retailers by August 2001, thanks in part to the imminent arrival of the Discovery Communications headquarters and its 1,500 expected employees.

In September 2002, construction began on a section that contains approximately 76,000 square feet (7,000 square meters) of retail and restaurant space, plus 63,000 square feet (6,000 square meters) of entertainment space in the AFI and Round House theaters. This section includes the rehabilitation of the historic shopping center at the corner of Georgia Avenue and Colesville Road. Renamed Gateway Plaza, the restored center once again displays its original colors of silver, sunshine yellow, mint green, coral pink, and sky blue. The restored Silver Theatre also lies within this block.

The former owners of the Silver Theatre, which opened in 1938 and closed in 1984, had demolished its art deco–style chimney and marquee tower in the early 1980s in an unsuccessful effort to

block the building from being designated as a historic structure. In 1996, Montgomery County acquired the theater; two years later, the county signed an agreement with AFI to restore the theater and to subsidize its operations. The cost of the restoration, originally estimated to run between $4 million and $5 million, eventually grew to nearly $24 million. Renamed the American Film Institute Silver Theatre and Cultural Center (AFI Silver), it reopened in April 2003, the culmination of a nearly 20-year effort. The county has leased the restored theater and related new facilities to AFI for the nominal sum of $10 per year for a ten-year period. Either party may terminate the initial lease at any time after the fifth year with one year's written notice. The agreement includes a provision for nine ten-year renewals.

The development team's longstanding desire to attract a mainstream multiplex cinema finally was realized when it signed an agreement with Consolidated Theatres in April 2002. In September 2002, ground was broken for a 20-screen, state-of-the-art movie complex on the southwest corner of Ellsworth Drive and Fenton Street in Section B. The Majestic Cinema 20—with its marquee,

ground-floor lobby, and second-story cinemas—opened in May 2004 and has consistently been one of the chain's highest-grossing outlets. The presence of the Majestic, along with AFI and the Round House Theatre, has transformed DSS into a regional arts and entertainment destination. Section B also contains more retail space—200,000 square feet (19,000 square meters), including a Borders bookstore and an ULTA Salon—than any other part of the project.

Tenants

Early in the planning process, development team members collaboratively selected the types of businesses they thought would make DSS an economic catalyst and would spur further redevelopment, including a grocery store, a hardware store, a bookstore, movie theaters, and restaurants. For the first section of the project to open, they focused on attracting neighborhood retail tenants. Among the first retail tenants to open were Strosniders Hardware, Fresh Fields (now

Opposite: Owned and restored by the county, the 1938 Silver Theatre is now home to the American Film Institute Silver Theatre and Cultural Center (AFI Silver).

Photograph by Julie D. Stern

Whole Foods Market), Next Day Blinds, Hollywood Video, and Baja Fresh. Other restaurant tenants include a variety of national chains, such as Romano's Macaroni Grill, Panera Bread, Redrock Canyon Grill, and Red Lobster; regional chains, such as Austin Grill, Potbelly Sandwich Works, and Lebanese Taverna; and local outlets, such as Ceviche, Thai at Silver Spring, and Adega Wine Cellars & Café.

Attracting retail tenants to an unproven downtown location was a challenge. The hardware store, in particular, initially was not eager to come in, and it took a lease at 40 percent of market rate to bring that store into the project. Early in the planning process, Peterson approached retail tenants in the company's other projects and asked what it would take to bring them to Silver Spring. The answer was that retail tenants wanted free parking—at the developer's expense—on evenings and weekends.

In April 2003, the ANA became the first office tenant to sign a lease at DSS, and it became the project's lead office tenant when the building opened in late summer 2004. The office tenants are the global headquarters of WorldSpace Incorporated, an international satellite services provider, and of the Association of Public Health Laboratories.

Civic Space

Downtown Silver Spring is the setting for a wide range of public- and merchant-sponsored performances, festivals, and other community events. DSS hosts annual events such as the Summer Concert Series, which is held on Saturday evenings from June to August on Silver Plaza, plus Halloween Spooktacular, which invites children to trick or treat throughout the project's stores. Holiday Fest, which is held in December, is a free event that welcomes shoppers and diners to kick off the holiday season with refreshments, strolling entertainment, in-store samplings, and more. Other events sponsored by DSS and its tenants include book signings at the Borders bookstore, as well as live music, food tasting, and informational presentations by other merchants.

The Silver Spring Urban District presents a free outdoor summer concert series known as "Silver Spring Swings." Other on-site events include the Magical Montgomery Cultural Fair, the

Silver Spring Under the Stars outdoor film festival, and an annual Thanksgiving parade. A farmer's market also is held on Fenton Street on Saturday mornings from June through October. DSS benefits from a continuing Montgomery County/Greater Silver Spring Chamber of Commerce marketing campaign that is designed to deliver the message that Silver Spring has "sprung" and is now the place to come for entertainment, dining, shopping, working, and living. The campaign has placed large red "U's" throughout DSS and the rest of the downtown area on light pole banners, signs, buses, and posters and on buttons worn by county staff members and business and community representatives. Funded by a partnership between the county and the chamber of commerce at a total cost of $165,000, the campaign also uses advertising and other means to spread the word about what is available in Silver Spring.

Opposite: After two unsuccessful attempts to redevelop the area, a public/private development partnership came together to create a gathering place for this urban community that features a traditional street format punctuated by two plazas and that integrates existing structures with new construction.

Courtesy of the Peterson Companies

Downtown Silver Spring

SILVER SPRING, MARYLAND
www.downtownsilverspring.com

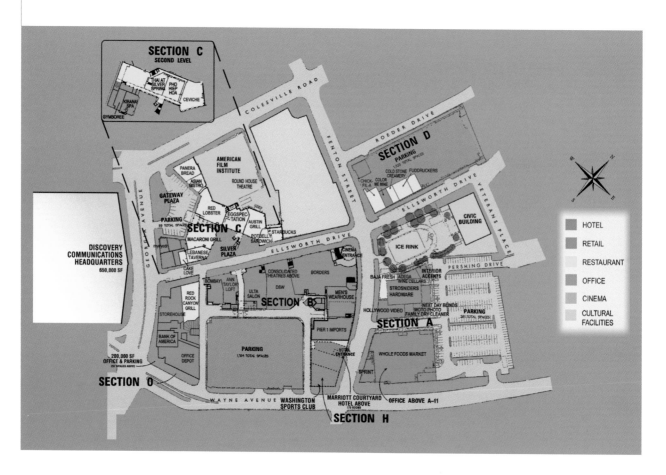

Site plan.

*Courtesy of the
Peterson Companies*

PROJECT TYPE

Town Center on a Redevelopment Site
Separate Owners
Site Area: 22 acres/8.9 hectares

LAND USE

Use	Square Feet	Number of Establishments/Units
Office:	185,000	
Retail:	440,000	
Hotel:	103,174	179
Public/Cultural Facilities:	67,000	
Parking:		3,858
Transit Linkages:		Regional Rail, Subway, Bus

DEVELOPMENT COSTS

Site Acquisition Cost (office and hotel FAR only):	$9,700,000
Soft Costs:	$27,380,000
Construction Costs (office and retail, by PFA):	$82,000,000
Total PFA Development Cost:	$120,000,000
Hotel Costs (funded by hotel owner):	$18,000,000
Tenant-Funded Improvement Costs (estimated):	$20,000,000
Future Residential Development Costs (estimated):	$70,000,000

DEVELOPMENT SCHEDULE

Planning Began:	April 1998
Ground Breaking:	May 1999
Phase I Complete:	June 2000
Town Center/Urban Village Buildout:	2008

DEVELOPMENT TEAM

Developers:

PFA Silver Spring, LC, a partnership among:

The Peterson Companies
Fairfax, Virginia
www.petersoncos.com

Foulger-Pratt
Rockville, Maryland
www.foulger-pratt.com

Argo Investment Company
Rockville, Maryland
www.argoinvestment.com

Master Planner:

RTKL
Washington, D.C.
www.rtkl.com

Architect:

BCT Architects
Baltimore, Maryland
www.bctarchitects.com

East 29th Avenue Town Center

DENVER, COLORADO

East 29th Avenue Town Center is one of four town centers at Stapleton, which is a master-planned community in Denver, Colorado, and was built on the site of the former Stapleton International Airport.

Photograph by Steve Larson

When the former Stapleton International Airport closed in 1995, Denver was confronted with the question of what to do with 4,700 acres (1,900 hectares) of vacant land in the center of the metro area.

The closing of the airport happened to coincide with the emergence of the new urbanist movement, which called for developing pedestrian-oriented neighborhoods with mixed uses. Although Denver has a reputation for being a sprawling western town, many of the city's older neighborhoods date back more than a century and were built along former streetcar lines. Many Denver residents saw new urbanism as a return to the characteristics of neighborhoods they cherished, including homes with front porches and garages on alleys. Most of Denver's old neighborhoods also have retail districts spanning a few blocks that rose up along the old streetcar lines.

One of those neighborhoods is Park Hill, which shares its eastern boundary with Stapleton at Quebec Street. As community discussion evolved over what to do with Stapleton, many people advocated using Park Hill as a model for redeveloping the airport.

"People wanted pedestrian-friendly retail of the kind you find in neighborhoods around Stapleton," said Tom Gleason, vice president of public relations for Forest City Stapleton, Inc.

The Stapleton Redevelopment Foundation was created in 1990 to guide the discussion, and it held dozens of town meetings. By the time the airport closed, the foundation had created a plan known as "the Green Book" that called for constructing a huge new urbanist community that would create mixed-use neighborhoods with homes for 30,000 residents and office space for 35,000 workers. That plan also called for the emergence of several "town centers" with pedestrian-oriented retail that would serve surrounding neighborhoods.

Forest City Enterprises was the master developer for the project and sought to create East 29th Avenue as an active, urban street that meshed with surrounding neighborhoods.

Courtesy of 360 Media

Design and Development

In 1998, Cleveland–based Forest City Enterprises was selected as Stapleton's master developer. In 2000, Forest City signed a purchase agreement to buy all 2,935 acres (1,188 hectares) of developable land at Stapleton. The land was then appraised at $79.4 million, but the price has increased with the rate of inflation as Forest City takes title to segments of the property over a 15-year time frame. The firm also pays a $15,000 fee per acre that is used to fund the development of parks and open space at Stapleton. Forest City has already purchased 1,200 acres (486 hectares) at the former airport.

Stapleton has quickly become a popular place for Denver residents to live, work, and shop. Stapleton is already home to 7,000 people. There is a growing amount of office space, and retail has also flourished.

The East 29th Avenue Town Center is the first of four planned town centers at Stapleton. The center opened in 2003 and was immediately a hit with residents. With nearly a dozen restaurants, an adjacent grocery store, and services ranging from a dentist to an animal hospital, the center brought intensive urban-style retail into the heart of Stapleton.

With office space and apartments on two floors above the ground-level retail shops, as well as hundreds of for sale and rental units that are just down the block, the street has a distinctly city vibe that has helped to differentiate Stapleton from suburban competitors. It has also reassured city residents that the huge development will be an extension of the urban fabric, while retaining characteristics of the surrounding neighborhoods.

Forest City wanted the East 29th Avenue Town Center to convey a message about Stapleton. "The initial development sets a tone," said Gleason. "We wanted to send a message that what we were doing was very urban in character. We wanted to create an active street scene."

Most of the retail shops along East 29th Avenue are situated on a narrow, two-lane segment of the street that extends for one and a half blocks. Parking is available behind the buildings. At the end of the second block, the street opens up around an oval park known as Founder's Green. The park features a water fountain, stone sculptures, and a large lawn that is the site of numerous community events.

The town center, which takes up 21.1 acres (8.5 hectares), includes 108,000 square feet (10,000 square meters) of office space, 140,000 square feet (13,000 square meters) of retail shops, and 66 units of market-rate rental above the retail stores.

The retail square footage includes a King Soopers grocery store and a Walgreens drug store that are built adjacent to the parking lots that lie behind the East 29th Avenue storefronts. Dozens of

Retail is clustered along one and a half blocks on East 29th Avenue, thus keeping in line with the overall density and walkability of the Stapleton development.

Courtesy of 360 Media

stores crowd the busy two blocks at the heart of the town center. A Stapleton visitor's center and real estate sales offices also have streetside space.

The retail at the town center has been hugely successful. "We are presently about 99 percent leased in the town center, which indicates a very positive response," said Gleason. Retail rental rates range from $25 to $45 per square foot.

Although many of the restaurants are national chains, including Starbucks and Chipotle Mexican Grill, Forest City made an effort to attract small local restaurants as well. Two of them, Udi's Bread Bistro and the Coral Room, have become known for their innovative menus. Many of the restaurants attract crowds for both lunch and dinner, and outdoor tables line the avenue.

There are several retail stores, including a boutique, a florist, a children's bookstore, and an ice cream shop.

Office tenants include a 14,000-square-foot (1,300-square-meter) pediatric clinic. A 34,000-square-foot (3,200-square-meter) medical office building is a key part of the town center. About 77 percent of the total office space in the town center is leased, with most of the available space being in

The development emphasizes its walkable, tree-lined streets and neighborhood stores.

Courtesy of 360 Media

Opposite: Sidewalk seating at restaurants is the retail parallel of front porches on houses.

Courtesy of 360 Media

the medical building. About 20,000 square feet (1,900 square meters) of the medical space is still for rent, with an asking price of $21.50 per square foot.

According to Gleason, Forest City arranged private financing to build the town center. The Denver office of 4240 Architecture Inc. designed the project, which is mostly masonry with large expanses of windows.

The Founder's Green is an open space that is a vital part of the town center. The 2.5-acre (1.0-hectare) park includes an amphitheater that can accommodate 3,000 people and that is a popular venue for a host of community activities. Free outdoor movies are shown during "Stapleton Under the Stars." The park also hosts an open-air antique and art market known as the "Sweet William Market on the Green" and a weekly farmer's market held every Sunday between June and late September.

Every 4th of July, a community celebration known as "Founder's Day" is held at the park to celebrate both the founding of the country and the founders of Stapleton. Those events have helped to generate a strong sense of community within Stapleton.

"We have a lot of our festivals on the town green," said Gleason. He added that several thousand people turned out for the first Founder's Day and that he was thrilled to discover that most of them walked from the surrounding neighborhoods. "The event was just jammed, but the parking lots were empty," he said.

Most of the housing that is part of the town center is situated around Founder's Green. There are 66 units of market-rate rental housing in the Crescent Flats, which are located above the retail on East 29th Avenue. Approximately 85 percent of those apartments are leased.

Several housing developments line the east side of the park and directly face Founder's Green. They include the Botanica on the Green apartments and the Moda Lofts, which is currently under construction. Additionally, several large projects are within a block of the town center, including 100 units of senior housing at Clyburn at Stapleton and 80 units of income-restricted for-sale units at Roslyn Court. "What we're doing is giving people a range of choices around the green," said Gleason.

The Next Step

Plans are now underway for Stapleton's second town center in new neighborhoods that have recently been constructed on the east side of the old airport. The new town center will be known as Eastbridge, but this development will be smaller than the East 29th Avenue Town Center. The buildings will be single-story, but the center will also feature outdoor space for community gatherings.

Gleason said Forest City Stapleton has tried to learn from the experience of creating the East 29th Avenue center. Stapleton has attracted a large number of young families, and, at times, the sidewalks of the town center are filled with strollers. The next town center will have wider sidewalks to accommodate both outdoor dining and people who push strollers. "You want to make it possible for people to bring their kids in a stroller," said Gleason, adding there would also be space available for people to lock up strollers while they go inside.

Dealing with traffic has been an issue. Two one-way streets bisect the Founder's Green, and there has been much discussion as to how many stop signs are appropriate and where they should be located. "The common theme is how do you make it comfortable for pedestrians," said Gleason.

Development at Stapleton has already started to shift north of I-70, where plans are underway to break ground on several new neighborhoods in the coming years. Two more town centers will be built in that area.

Gleason said that the town centers have become one of the things that draw people to Stapleton. "People can do some of their daily chores at the town center or go to the restaurants," he said. "They're places for people to walk and gather."

The 2.5-acre (1.0-hectare) park in the town center is a popular spot for a variety of community activities and events.

Photograph by Steve Larson

East 29th Avenue Town Center

DENVER, COLORADO
www.stapletondenver.com

Site plan.

*Courtesy of
360 Media*

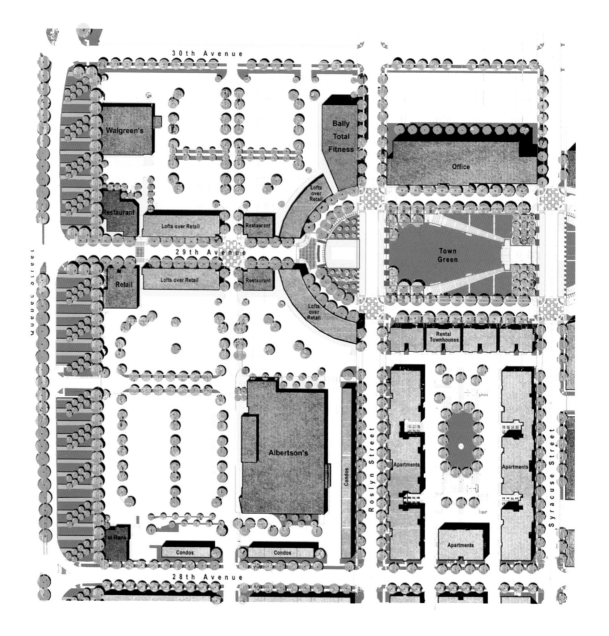

PROJECT TYPE

Town Center in a Master-Planned Community
Single Owner
Site Area: 21.1 acres/0.85 hectares

LAND USE

Use	Square Feet	Number of Establishments/Units
Office:	108,000	
Retail:	140,317	24+
Residential (rental):		66
Civic/Cultural/Other:	Town green to host civic celebrations	
Transit Linkages:	Bus	

DEVELOPMENT SCHEDULE

Planning Began:	August 2000
Ground Breaking:	August 2000
Town Center/Urban Village Buildout:	2003

DEVELOPMENT TEAM

Developer:

Forest City Stapleton
Denver, Colorado
www.forestcity.net

Owner:

Forest City Stapleton
Denver, Colorado
www.forestcity.net

Master Planner:

Forest City Stapleton
Denver, Colorado
www.forestcity.net

Architect:

4240 Architecture, Inc.
Denver, Colorado
www.4240architecture.com

Landscape Architect:

Nuszer Kopatz
Denver, Colorado
www.nuszer-kopatz.com

Engineer:

S. A. Miro Consulting Engineers
Denver, Colorado
www.samiro.com

Environmental Graphic Designer:

Communication Arts
Boulder, Colorado
www.commartsdesign.com

Market Researcher:

Forest City
Denver, Colorado
www.forestcity.net

Public Partners:

City and County of Denver
Denver, Colorado
www.denvergov.org

Excelsior and Grand

ST. LOUIS PARK, MINNESOTA

Seeking to create a town center, the city of St. Louis Park, Minnesota, entered a public/private partnership with TOLD Development Company to develop Excelsior and Grand. The $150 million mixed-use project occupies 16 acres (6.5 hectares) and contains apartments, condominiums, retail space, and a town green that links to an existing city park.

Designed by Elness Swenson Graham Architects, Inc. (ESG), this four-phase project consists of 88,000 square feet (8,200 square meters) of retail space, 338 apartments, and 306 for-sale condominiums. Furthermore, it provides the city of St. Louis Park, which is a first-ring suburb west of Minneapolis, with a pedestrian-friendly downtown.

Development Background

The planning for Excelsior and Grand dates back to the mid-1990s, when the city of St. Louis Park began a visioning process to address a variety of issues. One of the city's desires was to establish a sense of community and connectivity, and the creation of a mixed-use town center fit that vision. It was determined (a) that the 16 acres (6.5 hectares) of present-day Excelsior and Grand was the most underused area in the Park Commons and (b) that developing a variety of residential, retail, office, and open spaces and improving adjacent Wolfe Park would be an appropriate use of public funds and effort.

At the time, the portion of the site along Excelsior Boulevard was lined with blighted single-use properties that housed various businesses, including infamous bars, pawnshops, and other uses, that were generally unpopular within the community. Thus, the area was targeted for redevelopment.

In 1996, the city initiated a series of charrettes that were funded by the Metropolitan Council (the Twin Cities' regional governing body) Livable Communities Grant Program. That program helps local communities leverage their development plans. The charrettes brought prominent Twin Cities urban designers together to sketch plans for the Excelsior and Grand area, which was then called Park Commons East.

It was determined that Excelsior Boulevard, which runs along the southern border of the site, should be linked with the underused Wolfe Park, which lies to the north. A "town green" concept consisting of a large open space and a pedestrian area was created. As a major feature of the project, the town green concept would survive several iterations of the design.

The charrette process was combined with market studies of the retail and residential components, as well as pro formas to assess what uses and densities would be required to make the project financially feasible. This process informed the planners that densities would have to be increased from earlier designs. As a result, the town green was narrowed from 300 feet to 180 feet (90 meters to 55 meters), and the density was increased to contain four-story buildings.

The site previously consisted of 36 separate parcels, which contained a mix of commercial uses and single-family homes. The city began land assembly in the mid-1990s, acquiring all the sites by the end of 2000. It did not use eminent domain.

To ensure timely approvals for development at Excelsior and Grand, the city of St. Louis Park drafted an entirely new mixed-use zoning code (MX). Based on mixed-use and new urbanist projects around the United States, the zoning code allowed for things such as vertical mixed-use development and diagonal on-street parking.

Designed to create a pedestrian-friendly downtown, Excelsior and Grand is the result of a public/private partnership between the city of St. Louis Park and TOLD Development Company.

Heinrich Photography

Financing

Using a request for qualifications (RFQ) process, the city chose a developer in 1999. However, that relationship ended in 2000 because of external pressures requiring the developer to focus on its East and West Coast projects. Furthermore, the developer also had difficulty achieving a balanced pro forma for the project.

During a second, accelerated process, this time using a request for proposals (RFP), TOLD was selected within 45 days, mainly because of its experience with commercial development. ESG, which has substantial experience in designing residential properties, was retained by TOLD as project architect. Ground breaking on Phase I occurred in summer 2001.

The public involvement in the planning process continued after TOLD was selected to be the developer, with the company participating in more than 40 public meetings, as well as weekly meetings with city staff members. From this planning evolved the current master plan for Excelsior and Grand.

TOLD inherited a set of design standards, including mixed-use zoning code, with most approvals already in place and with traffic studies and environmental work that were also complete. The standards made the project very attractive to the developer, enabling it, together with the city, to focus on the difficult task of developing and financing the mixed-use project.

Several market studies revealed substantial potential for rental housing, retail, and office uses on the site. However, by 2001, the office and apartment markets had started showing signs of

St. Louis Park drafted a mixed-use zoning code (MX) to accommodate the project. The new code allows for features such as vertical mixed-use development and diagonal on-street parking.

Courtesy of ESG Architects, Inc.

weakening. Conversely, the condominium market began experiencing an upswing; as a result, office uses that were planned for later phases were converted to condominiums.

Financing for the project came from numerous public and private sources. Approximately 20 percent of the financing, or $30 million of the $150-million project cost, was derived from public sources. The Metropolitan Council Livable Communities Grant Program funded the charrette process and the initial market studies, and the Minnesota Department of Trade and Economic Development provided funding for the demolition of existing structures. Very little site cleanup or soil contamination was associated with the project. A tax increment financing (TIF) district, which was created for the area in 1978, assisted the city with the cost of land assembly.

The town green sits nestled between the four-story, mixed-use buildings. This open space links Excelsior and Grand to Wolfe Park, a city-owned recreational area.

Courtesy of ESG Architects, Inc.

Design and Planning

The original plan that was created by the previous developer contained the town green concept, but the buildings were on larger blocks, had much more retail space, and included surface parking behind the structures. When TOLD was selected to be the developer in 2000, the overall consensus was to break up the blocks into smaller, more intimate pieces; to reduce the amount of retail space, which would serve a more local clientele; and to hide as much parking as possible either underground or in ramps behind buildings.

TOLD stressed that the project needed to have a "sense of place" and not be just another collection of disparate uses with underused open space. The overall Excelsior and Grand master plan, which is a collaborative effort by TOLD, ESG, and landscape architecture firm Damon Farber Associates, emphasizes a vertical mix of uses in an architecturally varied and well-integrated streetscape that is intended to weave the development together.

The land use plan for Excelsior and Grand can be broken into five blocks, three of which have frontage on Excelsior Boulevard, and two that overlook Wolfe Park. The town green concept (now called Grand Way) is the "Main Street" of the project. At 2.1 acres (0.85 hectare), it is designed to invite interaction, to inspire strolling, and to play host to public events. Lined largely by retail uses

Lined largely by retail uses at the ground level, the town green includes a wide median with walking paths, benches, fountains, public art, and plantings.

Heinrich Photography

124

at the ground level, the project features wide, brick-paved sidewalks; outdoor seating for restaurants in the warmer months; decorative lampposts; kiosks; and elevated crosswalks. It also includes a wide median with walking paths, benches, fountains, public art, and plantings.

Phase I of Excelsior and Grand comprises two nearly symmetrical blocks of mixed-use development, which is bisected by Grand Way. Four-story buildings face Grand Way, with retail space on the main floor and with three stories of apartments above. When one moves away from Grand Way in either direction, the retail buildings are followed by parking structures and then by four-story U-shaped buildings that surround courtyards. These U-shaped buildings are entirely residential with the exception of first-floor retail uses in front of Excelsior Boulevard.

Although public space and a pedestrian-oriented environment are heavily emphasized design elements, the apartment buildings also have a significant amount of private space and amenities for the use of residents only. Renters have access to an on-site outdoor pool, a party room, and health facilities, and the two blocks each contain landscaped interior courtyards.

For financing purposes, it was decided that Phase I would contain more than half of the residential units, more than two-thirds of the retail space, and all of the off-street structured parking for the entire Excelsior and Grand project. Creating a critical mass of leasable space helped to leverage the public and private funding for the project.

From a marketing standpoint, finishing Grand Way and the buildings along Excelsior Boulevard, as well as a majority of the retail space, conveyed the impression that the development was largely completed. It created significant press coverage and a buzz within the community that this project was indeed significant for the Twin Cities.

Structures fronting Excelsior Boulevard and Grand Way are four stories high, with retail space on the ground floor and apartments above that level. Two "crowns" adorn the rooftops of the buildings opposite each other at Excelsior Boulevard and Grand Way. Those crowns help form an entry "monument" to the project and are visually distinctive from the Excelsior Boulevard perspective.

Retail space was placed along Excelsior Boulevard because it has substantial drive-by traffic and along Grand Way because it was designed to be the focal point for pedestrian traffic and has signalized access for automobiles. Park Commons Drive is mostly lined with residential units at street level. Those units are largely designed with direct outside access, as well as hallway access. The front doors and stoops help to create a more tranquil streetscape for the area.

Parking is hidden as much as possible; ramps are used to access the underground with entrances on Excelsior Boulevard and Park Commons Drive. The parking structures were designed to create minimal disruption on sidewalks and in building façades, and yet they are prominently marked to make it easy for drivers to find them.

In the development are a total of 1,090 parking spaces. The two parking structures together contain 470 parking stalls. Approximately 400 spaces are located underground for apartment residents, and the remaining 220 spaces are located above ground and are free for visitors. On-street parking is found on all streets within Excelsior and Grand, which is maximized by diagonal parking on Grand Way. A parking study determined the number of stalls based on peak hours of all uses, including events that are held at adjacent Wolfe Park.

Tenants and Performance

Leasing at Excelsior and Grand has been successful. Despite a weak Twin Cities rental market at the time of the opening, the apartments have performed ahead of expectations. The first rental building opened in December 2002, with the second and third opening in the spring and summer of 2003, respectively. All three buildings were entirely leased within 90 days, and the fourth, which opened in the fall of 2003, was fully leased within six months. TOLD expressed surprise at the renter profile, which was slightly older than expected, with some tenants in their 50s. This profile may be because of the high monthly rents that are charged for some units and can run as high as $3,600.

Of the 338 rental units, 18 are designated affordable under the Section 8 Housing Program. Leasing and management of the apartments were originally handled by Great Lakes Management. TOLD Development Company has since assumed management of the project.

National tenants such as Starbucks, Cold Stone Creamery, and Panera Bread signed leases for the retail space. This process is handled by Grubb & Ellis. Typical leases at Excelsior and Grand range from $20 to $32 per square foot ($215.30 to $344.50 per square meter). Trader Joe's occupies a 14,000-square-foot (1,300-square-meter) street-level retail space in the Phase III building. One tenant, Snyder's Drug, vacated its space because of the bankruptcy of its parent company; however, Pier One Imports signed a lease in early 2005 and filled the space.

Coinciding with the development of Excelsior and Grand, the city invested in upgrading the underused Wolfe Park. The creation of Grand Way provided a major connection to and exposure for the park, and the city built a band shell, pavilion, and playground in 2004, as well as improving sidewalks and pathways.

The portion of Grand Way to the north of Park Commons Drive is designed in a manner that allows it to be closed off for festivals and activities without disrupting traffic access to Excelsior and Grand parking. During the warmer months, a farmer's market is held on this portion of the street. Proving to be popular with area residents, the activities that are planned in Wolfe Park and on Grand Way help to bring people to the area and increase public activity.

Reasons It Works

The design of Excelsior and Grand mixes uses vertically and provides pedestrian-oriented public space while accommodating the needs of the automobile. Because of its design, the development has become both a popular destination and a place to live.

Because Excelsior Boulevard is a county road, a particular challenge was to gain approval from the county for installing a traffic signal at the intersection of Grand Way. A traffic signal was absolutely necessary for vehicles to access the project from both directions; the entire master plan relied on it, but the county was concerned that it would disrupt traffic flow. One of the county com-

Named after the intersection on which it is situated, Excelsior and Grand is a 16-acre (6.5-hectare), mixed-use project located in St. Louis Park, which is a first-ring suburb of Minneapolis, Minnesota.

Heinrich Photography

missioners, who is a former mayor of St. Louis Park, played a critical role in gaining county approval for the new traffic signal.

The willingness of the entire development team, including the city, to create a vision and to implement it through an open, transparent process was at the heart of Excelsior and Grand's success. Municipal officials state that the "stars aligned" for the project, not only because of the public will and vision to see blighted properties redeveloped, but also because of the availability of public money for planning and project financing and a development team that was willing to try something riskier than a more traditional project. However, representatives from TOLD Development note that recent changes to TIF laws in Minnesota will restrict the potential for future projects like Excelsior and Grand, as well as that other sources of necessary public money will need to be found.

Not only did the stars align for the creation of Excelsior and Grand, but also the site was well chosen. The project's location along a high-traffic arterial helps with not just retail visibility, but also overall marketing. It has been noted that some of the retailers were initially concerned about the limited number of parking spaces directly outside their door, but high traffic counts and a strong daytime population have bolstered demand for the retail uses. Furthermore, the residential development adds to the housing choices in the area.

Perhaps the key aspect of the success of the entire project was public support. The extensive public visioning process, which began fully six years before ground breaking, ensured that the development met with community approval.

The Veterans' Memorial Amphitheater is the focal point at the terminus of the town green.

Photograph by Sam Newberg

Excelsior and Grand

ST. LOUIS PARK, MINNESOTA
www.excelsiorandgrand.com

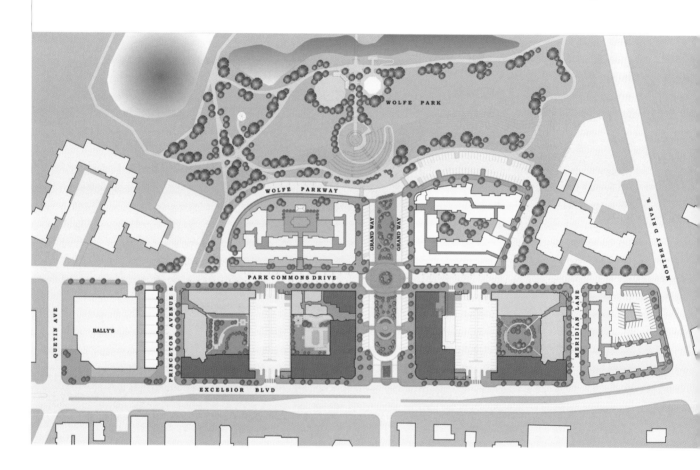

Site plan.

*Courtesy of ESG
Architects, Inc.*

PROJECT TYPE

Urban Village on a Redevelopment Site
Single Owner
Site Area: 16 acres/6.5 hectares

LAND USE

Use	Square Feet	Number of Establishments/Units
Retail:	88,000	16
Residential:	416,000	644
Parking:		1,090
Transit Linkages:		Bus

DEVELOPMENT COSTS

Total Town Center/Urban Village
Development Cost: $150,000,000

DEVELOPMENT SCHEDULE

Planning Began:	1995
Ground Breaking:	2001
Phase I Complete:	2003
Phase II Complete:	2005
Phase III Compete:	2006
Phase IV Complete:	2007

DEVELOPMENT TEAM

Developer:
TOLD Development Company
Plymouth, Minnesota
www.tolddevelopmentcompany.com

Master Planner:
ESG Architects
Minneapolis, Minnesota
www.esgarch.com

Architect:
ESG Architects
Minneapolis, Minnesota
www.esgarch.com

Landscape Architect:
Damon Farber Associates
Minneapolis, Minnesota
www.damonfarber.com

Construction Firm:
BOR-SON Construction, Inc.
Minneapolis, Minnesota
www.borson.com

The Glen Town Center

As a portion of the redevelopment of the Glenview Naval
Air Station, the Glen Town Center is a mixed-use project with retail, restaurants, entertainment, and housing that provides a village core for the city of Glenview, Illinois. San Diego–based Oliver McMillan developed the project, working closely with the village of Glenview, which is a suburb located north of Chicago.

With 473,000 square feet (44,000 square meters) of retail, restaurant, and entertainment space, plus 181 apartment units and 154 townhouses on a 45-acre (18.2-hectare) site, the Glen Town Center has become a successful mixed-use center for the village of Glenview. This success is in spite of a crowded field of major retail destinations in the northern Chicago suburbs.

The historical air base hangar and tower—a focal point of the development—was renovated to accommodate ground-level retail.

Courtesy of OliverMcMillan

History and Approvals

The Glenview Naval Air Station closed in 1995, leaving an unused 1,181-acre (478-hectare) parcel in the middle of the city of Glenview. The city immediately began redevelopment plans, hiring Skidmore, Owings & Merrill to create a master plan for the site.

The resulting plan and design guidelines include residential neighborhoods, two senior housing developments, a new Metro commuter rail station, two retail centers, more than 100 acres (40.5 hectares) of parks and open space, two golf courses, a children's museum, two public schools, and a mixed-use town center. In 2000, OliverMcMillan won a request for proposals (RFP) among a field of several experienced firms and was chosen to be the developer of the mixed-use town center.

The village of Glenview determined that the one significant building to preserve from the original base was Hangar One, which is a 1929 structure consisting of a hangar and control tower. It actually predated the Navy's use of the airfield, which began in 1937. The location of Hangar One was the determining factor for the siting of the mixed-use town center, which was planned around the building.

Planning for the Glen Town Center began in 2000: in December of that year, Von Maur signed a letter of intent for a 160,000-square-foot (15,000-square-meter) store, making that department store

CREATING GREAT TOWN CENTERS AND URBAN VILLAGES

the lead anchor tenant. The 9/11 attacks affected several tenants' decision to open a store at the town center and also threatened the financing of the project. As a result, OliverMcMillan provided a greater share of the equity, moving the project ahead. The grand opening occurred in October 2003.

Challenges

A significant challenge for the Glen Town Center is its location. Because of the decision to preserve Hangar One, which is located at the middle of the site, the town center is not located on a major road. Willow Road and Lake Avenue are east/west arterials that flank the town center on the north and south, respectively. Connecting the two is Patriot Drive, which is an entirely new road crossing the Glen Town Center from north to south.

Ideally, the Glen Town Center should have been located along Willow Road or Lake Avenue to capture the highest traffic counts. In fact, two retail nodes are indeed located along those roads as

part of the town center. The location of Hangar One at the middle of the site, which is just off Patriot Drive, and its inclusion in the town center plan dictated the location of the Glen Town Center. OliverMcMillan has made up for this limited drive-by traffic by offering a variety of retailers and an urban village environment that is not offered elsewhere in the region.

Although it was a priority for the city and developer to preserve Hangar One, it was certainly a challenge to achieve. Even though it was listed on the National Historic Register, the building, which dated to 1929, could have been demolished if a feasible use were not found. OliverMcMillan believed saving it was the right thing to do, and the city agreed to provide $10 million in assistance to do so. Retailers operate out of the ground floor of the old Hangar One building, which is seamlessly integrated into the new buildings surrounding it. The tower itself is the focal point and centerpiece of the project.

Housing over retail stores helps create higher density in this mixed-use development.

Courtesy of OliverMcMillan

Overall, the city invested $76.5 million in the project, using tax-increment financing (TIF). The TIF was used for street and parking structure construction, both of which were subsequently deeded back to the city. The TIF is also offset by the $21.6 million paid to the city by the developer for the site, and $17 million in revenue-sharing between the city and several tenants. The assessed value of the completed project is more than $500 million, and the return on investment to the developer has been 11 percent

Design

Especially in light of its location away from major roadways, the fundamental key to the success of the Glen Town Center is an attractive urban design that draws people and activity. To create a high-quality design for the project, OliverMcMillan convened a charette with notable firms such as

Gensler; Pappageorge Haymes; Ehrenkrantz, Eckstut & Kuhn; and Benson and Bohl. Gensler and Pappageorge Haymes were later retained to design the town center buildings.

The Glen Town Center's main street, Tower Drive, was originally the air strip on which the Navy planes took off and landed.

Courtesy of OliverMcMillan

The result of the charette was a town center plan that laid out a curved, pedestrian-oriented main street called Tower Drive that ran in front of Hangar One. The main focus of activity in the project is along Tower Drive. Patriot Drive forms the eastern edge of the Glen Town Center, and it provides most of the traffic that feeds it. At nearly 100 acres (40.5 hectares), Gallery Park, which is a new city park, is located to the east. The Kohl Children's Museum is located to the north, a golf course is located to the west, and a variety of housing is located to the south of the site.

The city created an entirely new zoning code to accommodate the mix of uses at the Glen Town Center. The zoning, which is called Mixed-Use Retail Center (MURC), accommodates retail, restaurant, and entertainment uses in a mixed-use setting with multifamily residential, including rental apartments and for-sale townhouses. In 1999, the city also created the Glen Redevelopment Commission to handle planning, permitting, and approvals for the entire 1,181-acre (478-hectare) project.

Design guidelines that were created by Skidmore, Owings & Merrill were adhered to, with retail and restaurant storefronts facing wide sidewalks. Blank walls are discouraged, and large footprint stores contain street frontage but have most of their square footage behind smaller, liner shops.

Parking and loading docks are located off Tower Drive and behind buildings, with the exception of angled parking on street. To maintain the Hangar One tower as the tallest building on the site, designers limited building height to 45 feet (14 meters) in the town center.

The streetscape is attractive with wide sidewalks that include trees, benches, and public art. High-quality building materials are used, with red brink and slate-colored shakes that create a contrast to the light-tan bricks of Hangar One. The difference in building materials is intended to convey a sense that the project has evolved over time. This tactic is a common one for new town center development, although in this case some of the buildings are indeed historic even if Hangar One was not originally built for retail uses.

A total of 181 apartments are located above the retail storefronts along the east side of Tower Drive. The 154 townhouses are located at the north and south end of the town center, as well as a

Navy Park, the center of the project, is located directly in front of the former hangar and tower.

Courtesy of OliverMcMillan

few that face Patriot Drive on the east side of the apartment blocks. Both the apartments and town-houses performed well in the market.

Parking is in two large structures to the west of Tower Drive. The structures are convenient for access but are hidden behind the retail uses that front Tower Drive. Two additional smaller parking structures are located in the middle of the two blocks between Tower and Patriot Drive. On-street parking, which is mostly angled, is a highly sought-after option for shoppers. Overall, there are 2,406 parking spaces in the town center, or just more than five stalls per 1,000 square feet (93 square meters) of retail space.

Two five-point intersections were created at the north and south end of the town center. They provide easy access from Patriot Boulevard to Tower Drive and the parking structures. The main entrance, or "front door," to the project from Patriot Drive is located in the middle of the Glen Town Center. There, the access street splits to form Navy Park in the middle, which is located in the shadow of the original tower.

Although two small parks are located between Patriot and Tower Drive at both the north and south end of the site, the key open space is Navy Park. It forms the core of the project and contains a lawn, a fountain, and some benches; it hosts concerts during the summer months.

The history of the Glen Town Center as a Navy base is honored in many ways. The preservation of Hangar One is a key, but several plaques are located on buildings around the site that describe locations where base personnel were deployed or served. Navy Park features statues of sailors and Navy aviation personnel and brick pavers inscribed with the names of Navy officers and enlisted personnel.

Because of the location of the Glen Town Center, the tenant selection and recruitment process was critical to achieve the appropriate mix. Anchor tenants include a 160,000-square-foot (15,000-square-meter) Von Maur department store, an 80,000-square-foot (7,400-square-meter) Dick's Sporting Goods, and a ten-screen Crown Theater. Collectively, the restaurants act as additional anchors. An important factor with the restaurants, however, is that they are predominantly established brands with previously little or no presence in the Chicago area. This influx presents an advantage, because prospective customers must now come to the Glen Town Center, and their presence helps add to having a unique experience at the new center.

The two anchor tenants, Von Maur and Dick's Sporting Goods, are located on either side of the tower along the west side of Tower Drive at the center of the project facing Navy Park. The Crown Theater is along the same side of Tower Drive just to the south. Most restaurants and soft goods are located at the southern end of the town center, and the clothing, fashion, and home furniture are on the north. Although the location of most retailers creates good synergy, the developer would have spread restaurants more widely across the project and intends to do so as tenants crossover in the future.

Since the inception of the master plan for the Glen Town Center by Skidmore Owings & Merrill, Tower Drive was always considered to be the "main street" for the town center. The city and OliverMcMillan considered a significant retail component facing Patriot Drive, as well, but determined that the critical mass was not enough for retail to face two streets. As a result, townhouses and a couple restaurants are all that actually face Patriot Drive.

Parking in front of the mixed-use buildings provides a barrier between the sidewalks and the street.

Courtesy of OliverMcMillan

Lessons Learned

The Glen Town Center has been a success, with retail spaces and apartments that are both more than 95 percent leased and with townhouses that are sold out. Perhaps most important to the success has been the relationship between the developer and the city. OliverMcMillan credits the city for being progressive and for having a stable political environment, which has allowed the original vision and plan for the site to be achieved despite challenges along the way.

The project was effectively a single-phase development, despite having two grand openings: one in October 2003 and a second wave of stores in June 2004. However, the developer would have preferred the Glen Town Center to have opened in two or more phases. This scheduling was especially desirable given the circumstances following 9/11, which affected leases and the financing of the project, although not necessarily its timing.

The Glen Town Center

GLENVIEW, ILLINOIS
www.theglentowncenter.com

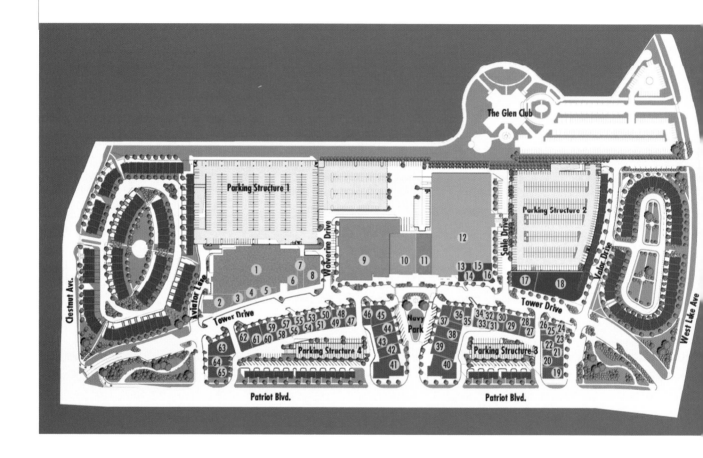

Site plan.

*Courtesy of
OliverMcMillan*

PROJECT TYPE

Town Center in a Master-Planned Community
Single Owner
Site Area: 45 acres/18.2 hectares

LAND USE

Use	Square Feet	Number of Establishments/Units
Retail:	473,206	
Residential:		335
Apartments:		181
Townhouses:		154
Parking:		2,406
Transit Linkages:		Regional Rail, Bus

DEVELOPMENT TEAM

Developer:
OliverMcMillan
San Diego, California
www.olivermcmillan.com

Owner:
OliverMcMillan
San Diego, California
www.olivermcmillan.com

Architects:
Gensler
Chicago, Illinois
www.gensler.com

Pappageorge Haymes
Chicago, Illinois
www.pappageorgehaymes.com

Benson & Bohl
San Diego, California
www.bensonbohl.com

Ehrenkrantz, Eckstut & Kuhn
New York, New York
www.eekarchitects.com

Landscape Architect:
Douglas Hoerr Landscape Architects
Chicago, Illinois
www.douglashoerr.com

Engineer:
Cowhey Gudmundson Leder, Ltd.
Chicago, Illinois
www.cgl-ltd.com

Environmental Graphic Designer:
Gensler
Chicago, Illinois
www.gensler.com

Market Researcher:
Tracy Cross & Associates, Inc.
Schaumburg, Illinois
www.tcrossinc.com

DEVELOPMENT COSTS

Total Town Center Development Cost: $140,000,000

DEVELOPMENT SCHEDULE

Planning Began: March 2001
Ground Breaking: October 2002
Town Center/Urban Village Buildout: October 2003

The Market Common, Clarendon

ARLINGTON, VIRGINIA

The Market Common, Clarendon, is a successful, mixed-use infill development that is located along the Rosslyn–Ballston metrorail corridor in Arlington, Virginia. The project blazed a path in attracting "suburban urbanites" with its relatively higher density, upscale shopping and its access to downtown Washington, D.C., jobs and transit. The developers, McCaffery Interests, Inc., transformed a former parking lot into a pedestrian friendly community that compliments the surrounding uses. The result was 303,000 square feet (28,000 square meters) of retail, 87 residential townhouses, and 300 apartments that all helped to revitalize the Clarendon neighborhood.

Since opening in November 2001, the 13.9-acre (5.6-hectare) Market Common has served as a model for compact, pedestrian-oriented development in surrounding areas. Within two years, 8,000 new residential units and 210,000 square feet (20,000 square meters) of Class A office space were under construction within a two-block radius of the Market Common. By 2007, projects that were either approved or were under review include 1,042 residential units, 300,000 square feet (28,000 square meters) of office space, and 200,000 square feet (19,000 square meters) of retail space.

The success of the Market Common is derived, in large part, from the developer's commitment to creating high-quality pedestrian environments. Founded in 1991, McCaffery Interests has developed mixed-use projects in diverse locations such as California, Illinois, and Pennsylvania, but its designers emphasize pedestrian access and appropriate scale for each project. The firm promotes the "lowest and best use" for a site, meaning that the firm eschews high-risk, large-scale projects in favor of lower risk, small-scale projects that pay careful attention to the needs and demands of the markets surrounding their sites. With the Market Common's six nationally known retail anchors (Crate & Barrel, Ann Taylor Loft, Barnes & Noble, Chico's, the Container Store, and Pottery Barn),

Housing units built over retail stores add greater density and synergy to the development.

Courtesy of McCaffery Interests, Inc.

the developer tapped into an underserved community's demand for high-end goods while simultaneously creating a walkable outdoor atmosphere.

Site and Development Process

The 13.9-acre (5.6-hectare) development of the Market Common consists of one superblock (Phase I) and two smaller parcels (Phases II and III). The Market Common Phase I, which is the largest, consists of a retail component and the housing. Directly across from Clarendon Boulevard is Phase II, which comprises a smaller block that originally held a Sears store and that now includes parking over retail. Phase III occupies the block to the west of Phase II and contains a Cheesecake Factory and La Tasca Tapas.

The project infused life into an area that was well located but had seen better days. Starting in

The Market Common, Clarendon, is an infill project that is pedestrian-friendly and is located close to a mass transit station.

Courtesy of Sisson Studios

the 1960s, Clarendon's small-scale retailers could no longer compete with the modern shopping malls at Tyson's Corner and nearby Seven Corners. The area lost its commercial appeal and fell into disrepair. In 1979, a metrorail line extended through Arlington in hopes of revitalizing the aging corridor. While neighboring Rosslyn and Ballston developed quickly because of nearby major high-ways, Clarendon had little new development and an overabundance of surface parking. However, the area was known for its bars, Vietnamese restaurants, and charming residential neighborhoods, which were gentrifying.

The rapid growth along the corridor was a concern for the residents in the surrounding area. In 1995, neighborhood residents said a Home Depot would not fit with the area's character, and the home-improvement chain withdrew its plan to open a store in Clarendon. The year before, the County Board rejected a proposed McDonald's restaurant. McCaffery Interests worked closely with

the residents to find mutually agreeable outcomes. Both parties wanted the site to be integrated into the surrounding neighborhood, with multiple points of entrance and egress. Both sides also wanted the project to be built at a pedestrian-friendly scale, with thoughtful design and placement of amenities. And they wanted high quality, nationally known retail tenants.

Townhouses line a small park at the rear of the project, thus connecting the development to existing residential neighborhoods.

Courtesy of McCaffery Interests, Inc.

Planning and Design

The project's proximity to a metrorail station and Arlington County's support of a denser development in the area provided the development team with a unique opportunity to create a pedestrian-friendly place with 24-hour uses. To get ideas for the project, Daniel McCaffery, the firm's founder, visited successful pedestrian-friendly developments and town centers nationwide. Of those he visited, Mizner Park in Boca Ration, Florida, was the main inspiration for the design of the Market Common, Clarendon.

The developer went through six months of planning meetings—40 meetings with neighborhood and community groups and 50 meetings with government agencies—before a plan emerged. The groups decided on an inward-facing retail center along Clarendon Boulevard and on placing some outward-facing housing along the three sides that are on residential streets. This design had no blank street façades and maximized the street frontage of the commercial center.

The central focus of the Market Common is a large, rectangular, landscaped courtyard in the center of Phase I. The courtyard includes a park with a bandstand shell, a small playground, a gazebo, and a fountain. At the front of the park is a garden with a water feature.

A one-way, two-lane street loops through the courtyard from Clarendon Boulevard. Both sides of the loop are lined with parallel parking spaces. The parallel parking adds to the urban character of the project, provides convenient parking for quick stops, and helps to calm traffic. The major retail component, with apartments overhead, encircles this street. Many of the larger stores occupy two levels, a configuration that was considered to be unworkable just a few years ago but is now embraced by many retailers.

The entrance to a shared parking garage is directly off the main loop. Shared parking minimizes the number of parking spaces required. About 1,000 structured parking spaces serve the entire development, including residents, shoppers, and others.

Phases II and III are located on the other side of Clarendon Boulevard. Two levels of parking sit atop the Phase II stores. Placing the parking garage above the street level allows storefronts to line the sidewalk along the entire block, an important design strategy for pedestrian-focused development. Market Place (Phase III) was a former auto-dominated area, which is now a thriving urban environment.

Small, well-placed developments, such as Phase II and the Market Place, can build on the success and synergy of much larger pedestrian-oriented projects. Small projects that offer appealing

The development is architecturally and socially focused on the large, rectangular, landscaped courtyard.

Courtesy of McCaffery Interests, Inc.

Walking paths and features such as a fountain draw pedestrians into the center of the Market Common.

Courtesy of McCaffery Interests, Inc.

routes and interesting destinations not only can take advantage of the foot traffic that is generated by larger projects, but also can contribute to it. The Whole Foods Market, at the northeastern end of the development, has many customers arriving by automobile, but the retailer reports one-third of the customers arrive on foot or by bicycle.

McCaffery Interests allowed some of the anchor tenants to hire their own architects. Street exposure was an effective form of marketing and brand identification for the retailers. By giving retailers a high degree of architectural autonomy, the development team not only helped support their marketing and branding efforts, but also created a rich and varied environment within a master-planned development. However, the development retains a visual cohesiveness by using the same bricks in the sidewalks that are used in the buildings and by using the sidewalks to tie together various aspects of the project.

The development team paid careful attention to finding the right combination of uses. Because the team believed that a strong residential component would create more street life and would give both the project and the surrounding commercial district a greater sense of vitality, the team chose to include more residential space than office space. As a result of the restaurants and residences, the area is still active long after the office-dominated areas nearby have closed.

Housing was integrated into the project with care and consideration. The 300 apartment units above the courtyard are a mixture of studios and one-, two- and three-bedroom units. To help create a greater sense of openness in the courtyard and to visually distinguish the apartments from the retail stores, the units are stepped back from the retail façade. The windows and balconies function as "eyes on the street" and create a sense of safety.

146

The 87 townhouses, which are developed by Eakin/Youngetob and designed by the Lessard Architectural Group, that flank the southern and eastern boundaries of the project were likewise planned with great care, and they help knit the project to the neighborhood. The placement of the townhouses creates a transition zone from the lower densities of the adjacent neighborhoods of single-family homes to the higher densities of the project. Pedestrian paths lead from the townhouses to the main courtyard, increasing the permeability of the Market Common and allowing neighboring residents to enter the development without them having to walk around the outer edges of the project.

A Unique Destination

The Market Common, Clarendon, proved that urban densities and amenities could work in a lower-density suburban environment. On the basis of its previous experience in building places for walking, the development team knew that people wanted inviting, safe, and interesting places to walk. Many of the project's residents wanted an access to public transportation and hoped to live within walking distance of retail stores, but they preferred to live outside the urban core. The Market Common gives consumers an option. By taking advantage of the existing pedestrian network, the developers enhanced it with an interesting design and added new routes to the network. By doing so, they created a unique destination that people can reach by foot, by public transit, and by car.

Stores and restaurants added in Phases II and III, and located across and along the Clarendon Boulevard corridor, further tie the project to the community.

Courtesy of McCaffery Interests, Inc.

The Market Common, Clarendon

ARLINGTON, VIRGINIA
www.marketcc.com

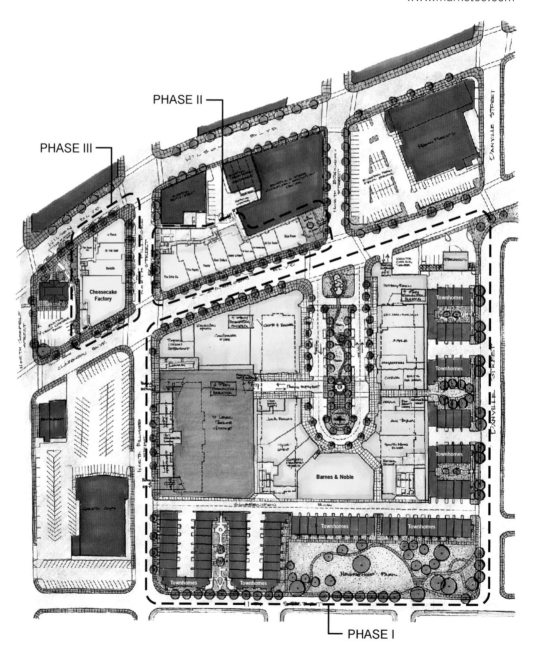

PHASE II

PHASE III

Cheesecake
Factory

Barnes & Noble

Townhomes

Townhomes

Townhomes

Townhomes

Townhomes

Townhomes

Townhomes

PHASE I

Site plan.

*Courtesy of
McCaffery
Interests, Inc.*

PROJECT TYPE

Urban Village on a Redevelopment Site
Single Owner
Site Area: 13.9 acres/5.6 hectares

LAND USE

Use	Square Feet	Number of Establishments/Units
Office:	92,900	
Retail:	266,000	39
Residential:		387
Apartments:		300
Townhomes:		87
Parking:		1,000
Transit Linkages:		Subway, Bus

DEVELOPMENT COSTS

Site Acquisition Cost:	$16,500,000
Site Improvement Cost:	$84,300,000
Soft Costs:	$25,000,000
Total Urban Village Development Cost:	$125,000,000

DEVELOPMENT SCHEDULE

Planning Began:	March 1999
Ground Breaking:	May 2000
Phase I Retail Complete:	November 2001
Phase I Residential Complete:	July 2002
Phases II and III Complete:	December 2003
Town Center/Urban Village Buildout:	December 2003

DEVELOPMENT TEAM

Developer:
McCaffery Interests, Inc.
Chicago, Illinois
www.mccafferyinterests.com

Development Partner:
RREEF
Chicago, Illinois
www.rreef.com

Master Planner:
Antunovich Associates
Chicago, Illinois
www.antunovich.com

Architect:
Antunovich Associates
Chicago, Illinois
www.antunovich.com

Landscape Architect:
Antunovich Associates
Chicago, Illinois
www.antunovich.com

General Contractors:
Plant Construction
San Francisco, California
www.plantco.com

Hensel-Phelps
Chantilly, Virginia
www.henselphillips.com

Residential Developer:
Eakin/Youngentob Associates
Bethesda, Maryland
www.eya.com

Financing Arrangements:
Downey Engrebretson
Minneapolis, Minnesota
www.downeyengebretson.com

River Ranch Town Center

LAFAYETTE, LOUISIANA

The Village of River Ranch represents a trend in town planning that has been growing over the past couple of decades: traditional neighborhood developments, or TNDs. These mixed-use throwbacks to pre–World War II times are popular for the proximity of retail space and office space to residential areas, thus creating pedestrian-friendly towns where people can work and run errands within the community. TNDs also contain amenities such as parks and civic space.

The town green ties the development together and provides a place for community events.

Courtesy of River Ranch Development Company, LLC

River Ranch Development Company and Steven Oubre, who spearheaded the project as the master planner and the principal architect, were the main forces behind the creation of the Village of River Ranch. The project is situated on a 324-acre (131.1-hectare) site located 4 miles (6.5 kilometers) from downtown Lafayette, Louisiana, a city with a population of 110,000 people. River Ranch contains 250,000 square feet (23,200 square meters) of retail, 200,000 square feet (18,600 square meters) of office space, a 51-room hotel, and 1,200 residential units. The 1,200 homes are split between apartments, condominiums, townhouses, and detached single family houses. At the heart of River Ranch is its Town Center, which is designed around a town green where community events are held throughout the year. Ground-level retail and upper-level residential create activity at the Town Center that spans the course of the day.

The Beginnings

Steven Oubre had been interested in TNDs since 1984—the year when he discovered the concept at a summer conference at Harvard University. Andrés Duany of DPZ (Duany Plater-Zyberk & Company) spoke at the conference about his Seaside development in Destiny, Florida. The Seaside project would prove to be the one that introduced TNDs to the world.

In the early 1990s, Oubre began seeking out possible locations for a TND in the greater Lafayette area and narrowed it down to about six places, including River Ranch, which had only recently

come onto the market. The city, however, had proposed a five-lane highway and a bridge that would cut through the River Ranch site. In response, the family of the former owner of the River Ranch property hired an attorney, Robert Daigle, to raise a lawsuit against the city to counter its proposal. Daigle, who happened to be a personal acquaintance of Oubre's, discussed with Oubre the possibility of building a TND on the land. Daigle took the suggestion to his clients, but they were reluctant to go forward at that time. Then, in 1996, the city had elected a new city-parish president, Walter Comeaux, in addition to several new council members. The tide had changed and city officials green-lighted the TND plan.

In September 1997, the River Ranch project got underway. During an early 1997 meeting at City Club, which is a 55,000-square-foot (5,000-square-meter) health and wellness center at River

River Ranch Town Center is located 4 miles (6.5 kilometers) from downtown Lafayette, Louisiana.

Courtesy of River Ranch Development Company, LLC

Ranch, the developers sold almost every lot in the first phase. This success spurred their decision to build out the first four residential phases at once. At the time, a small lot sold for about $6 per square foot with homes coming in at about $115 per square foot. Such affordable houses helped realize Oubre's and Daigle's goal of creating a mixed-income settlement.

A Center of Community Life

River Ranch Town Center, built around a town square on a village green, features retail shops, restaurants, and residences, and serves as a center of activity for community members. The town square, as a center of daily life, is a prime location for local businesses; a residential component is located on the upper levels. The annual Village Wine Festival and Spring Big Easel Art Festival take place in the town center. Retail shops and restaurants add variety and

Above: The town square, with its gazebo and village green, serves as a focal point in the town center. Left: Townhouses with first-floor retail line the side of the town square.

Courtesy of River Ranch Development Company, LLC

A design code that governs the aesthetics of River Ranch stipulates that bricks must be old and shutters must be functional. To ensure that construction will meet requirements, the development maintains a list of approved architects and builders.

Courtesy of River Ranch Development Company, LLC

interest as they extend activity into the evenings and weekends, and as they make the town square a destination not only for the residents of River Ranch, but also for the surrounding communities.

An integral part of the town center, the City Club at River Ranch is a 55,000-square-foot (5,100-square-meter) club with a full-service health and wellness center, a day spa, 13 tennis courts and a tennis pro shop, two swimming pools, a restaurant, a banquet room, and a business forum. Facing onto the town square itself, the City Club is ideally situated within walking distance of every residence.

Twenty-four townhouses front the town square as part of the Garden District. The townhouses were designed to accommodate individuals and families seeking the vibrant atmosphere of the town square, which is adorned with a gazebo and plays host to spontaneous gatherings and community events.

For visitors to the community, Carriage House Suites is located in the town center and offers 21 luxury suites in a stylish and intimate environment. Like residents of the community, guests benefit from the proximity of restaurants, spas, and shops.

A Familiar Setting

The Village of River Ranch physically lies in Lafayette, Louisiana, about 130 miles (210 kilometers) from New Orleans. However, some former residents of the Crescent City, who were displaced after Hurricane Katrina, have found that River Ranch reminds them of home, so much so that they have chosen to remain in River Ranch. Fixtures such as iron gates and balustrades, which feature details such as French horns in the design, are reminiscent of New Orleans in a way that appeals to some of the city's former residents.

Architectural details illustrate the strong New Orleans influence on River Ranch.

Courtesy of River Ranch Development Company, LLC

River Ranch developers acknowledge the strong New Orleans influence in the project's neighborhoods. One residential neighborhood, Uptown, was specifically built with New Orleans' Garden District in mind, and its mixing of French and Spanish architectural styles is evident in its neoclassical columns, wrought iron balconies, and courtyards with fountains. River Ranch's Crescent Apartments and the Rosewalk neighborhood are intended to emulate French Quarter architecture. Mill House condominiums look to the Warehouse District of New Orleans for design inspiration. The River Ranch Garden District takes its design cues from two New Orleans sources: the architecture of the district's garden homes ranges from the Urban Creole found in New Orleans' French Quarter to the Classical and Greek revival found in New Orleans' own Garden District.

The Village of River Ranch
and River Ranch Town Center

LAFAYETTE, LOUISIANA
www.riverranchdevelopment.com

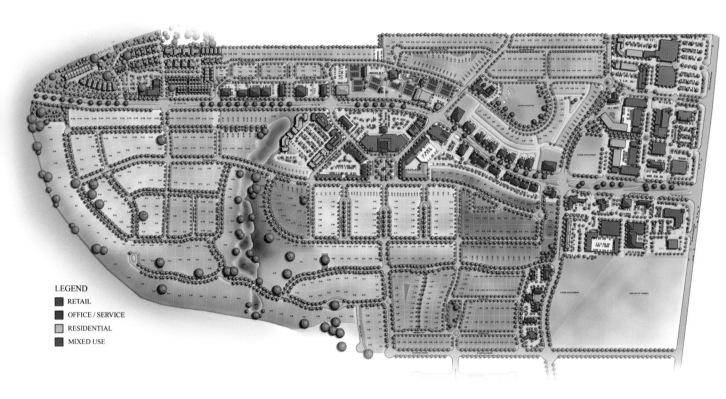

LEGEND
- RETAIL
- OFFICE / SERVICE
- RESIDENTIAL
- MIXED USE

Village site plan.

*Courtesy of River
Ranch Development
Company, LLC*

PROJECT TYPE

Town Center in a Master-Planned Community
Separate Owners
Site Area: 324 acres/131.1 hectares

LAND USE

Use	Square Feet	Number of Establishments/Units
Office:	85,000	
Retail:	71,000	
Residential (rentals, condos, and townhouses):		257
Services:	29,000	6
Hotel:		21
Transit Linkages:		Bus

DEVELOPMENT COSTS

Site Acquisition Cost:	$1,800,000
Site Improvement Cost:	$2,250,000
Soft Costs:	$425,000
Vertical Construction/Development Costs:	$61,600,000
Total Town Center Development Cost:	$66,075,000

DEVELOPMENT SCHEDULE

Planning Began:	June 1996
Ground Breaking:	September 1997
Phase I Complete:	1998
Phase II Complete:	2000
Phases III & IV Complete:	2002
Phase V Complete:	2004
Phase VI Complete:	2005
Town Center Buildout:	2007

DEVELOPMENT TEAM

Developer:
River Ranch Development Company, LLC
Lafayette, Louisiana
www.riverranchdevelopment.com

Owner:
River Ranch Development Company, LLC
Lafayette, Louisiana
www.riverranchdevelopment.com

Master Planner:
Steven J. Oubre, AIA
Architects Southwest
Lafayette, Louisiana
www.architectssouthwest.com

Architects:
Architects Southwest
Lafayette, Louisiana
www.architectssouthwest.com

Pecot & Company Architects
Lafayette, Louisiana
www.pecotarchitects.com

Park Design Group, LLC
New Orleans, Louisiana

Davis Designs
Lafayette, Louisiana

Landscape Architects:
Viator & Associates
Lafayette, Louisiana

Land Architecture, LLC
Lafayette, Louisiana
www.landarchitecture.net

Engineer:
Barry J. Bleichner, PE, PLS
Lafayette, Louisiana

Public Partner:
City of Lafayette
Lafayette, Louisiana
www.cityoflafayette.com

Santana Row

SAN JOSE, CALIFORNIA

Federal Realty Investment Trust's Santana Row is a mixed-use urban village of residential units, restaurants, shops, and a hotel that are located around a main street. The development's multistory yet low-rise buildings surround the outdoor open spaces that are adorned with public artwork. When the project is complete, Santana Row will comprise 680,000 square feet (63,000 square meters) of retail space and restaurants, 1,201 dwelling units, two hotels, and seven parks covering an 18-block area. This greyfield redevelopment project replaced a 1960s-era, single-story, suburban shopping center that was composed of ten buildings that were surrounded by sprawling parking lots, creating a high-density, multistory, mixed-use neighborhood in its place.

Though tailored for the project's particular setting and locale, the vision for Santana Row evolved from Federal Realty's previous experience in building Bethesda Row, which was an earlier mixed-use project in downtown Bethesda, Maryland. Buoyed by its success, Federal Realty was able to explore the concept of mixed-use developments on a much grander scale on the West Coast. The concept behind Santana Row originated from a combination of extensive research into both regional and European destination streets; an examination of local, historic, economic, and cultural trends; the area's vernacular architecture; and the lessons that had been learned from building Bethesda Row.

To achieve this concept, Santana Row needed the right balance of features to attract and to retain both residential and retail market share. Focusing on an upscale market, Federal Realty sought to combine high-quality rental housing that would fill a void in the Silicon Valley's real estate market with high-end fashion and lifestyle retailers that are not found elsewhere in the Bay Area. The overall goal was to create a lively, pedestrian-oriented atmosphere that offers a sense of discovery and adventure in a comfortable and safe environment. Anticipating eventual conversion, the developer had all of the residential rental units "condo mapped" at the outset, thus providing the flexibility to market them either as rentals or as a turnkey condominium conversion at any time. In 2005, the developer converted more than 200 units into condominiums, with all of the units selling briskly.

The developer was able to overcome several major setbacks before the opening in 2002. First, the bottom dropped out of the high-tech industry around the time that construction of Phase I began. Silicon Valley's economy was hit hard: companies were closed, jobs were lost, and people left the region. Then, the terrorist attacks of September 11, 2001, cast further doubt on the country's economic vitality by crippling the travel and tourism industry, by impeding retail sales, and by slowing down speculative business ventures. Finally, just 30 days before the originally scheduled grand opening, a devastating $100 million, eight-alarm fire destroyed the Santana Heights building, which was the largest of nine on the site at that time. The nearly completed structure had covered 6 acres (2.4 hectares) and had consisted of four floors of stores and luxury apartments above an underground garage. Thirty-six shops in various stages of construction and 242 townhouses and flats were destroyed.

Solutions were timely and pragmatic. Federal Realty faced the economic decline head on by reducing the average rent on residential units from an anticipated $3.07 per square foot to $2.05 per square foot and by negotiating creative lease terms with retail tenants to obviate risk, such as shorter terms and kick-out plans that were based on sales volume. In an even more unusual move, the real estate investment trust (REIT) became an investor in six restaurants in order to help them achieve successful, on-time openings. Insurance covered the damages, and rebuilding began almost immediately.

Many of Santana Row's shops, restaurants, and housing are oriented around a main street and linear park.

Photograph by Jay Graham, courtesy of SB Architects

Approvals

Federal Realty's plan was to raze the site and to redesign it from the subsurface up in order to accommodate Santana Row's large-scale program and to achieve optimal connections with surrounding neighborhoods and infrastructure. By early 1998, the concept was submitted to the city of San Jose as a general development plan (GDP). The GDP recognized that current zoning ordinances would have to be rewritten to accommodate a fully integrated, mixed-use urban design concept in a suburban setting. The specific plan was entitled in June 1998. From 1999 to 2003, numerous other major entitlements were received that supported the unique aspects of this planned unit development (PUD).

The public interaction process was elaborate. Most of the attendants at public hearings were neighborhood residents who kept up with the project through a dedicated Web site and newsletter and who collaborated with Federal Realty on finding solutions to their concerns. The developer also satisfied various environmental requirements, including relocating an endangered species of burrowing owl, moving and replanting 17 50-year-old oak trees at a cost of $30,000 per tree, and controlling outdoor lighting to prevent interference with the operations of Lick Observatory.

High-end retail shops and boutiques are located on the main street for the greatest exposure to pedestrian and vehicular traffic.

Photograph by Jennifer LeFurgy

Federal Realty was also faced with finding solutions to suburban zoning ordinances that did not apply to a project that was governed by urban design principles. Among other things, Federal Realty obtained approvals for shared parking between uses; redefined the parameters for parks and open space to fit project context; and rewrote the local lighting, signage, and graphics ordinance.

Planning and Design

The planning process began at the macro level; big decisions were made first. Maximum density and floor to area ratios were established on the basis of the findings of a traffic study that evaluated existing roadway volume capacity. Grids were used both to organize streets and blocks and to create a sense of structure around the retail and residential spaces. To allow for the greatest flexibility in apportioning retail and residential space, blocks were initially designed on a 30-foot-by-30-foot (9-meter-by-9-meter) structural grid.

The streets within this grid vary in both size and prominence, with Santana Row and Olin Avenue being the main streets. Wide sidewalks that are adorned with outdoor seating for restaurants and cafés are intended to give the main street a sense of vibrancy, and the developers set it up as a promenade for strolling. Landscaped medians stretch the length of the main street, and at one end of the project (between Olin Avenue and Olsen Drive), inside a wider median, lies Santana Row Park.

On each side of Santana Row Park, the street is lined with shops. The residential units of the Serrano and Santana Heights buildings sit atop and behind the shops on their respective sides of the street. Further down the main street, the residential units of the Villa Comet, the DeForest, and the Margo also sit atop high-end shops. In the middle of Santana Row, between Olin Avenue and Tatum Lane, is the Hotel Valencia. Like the other buildings along the main street, the ground floor is devoted to fashionable retail establishments and restaurants with the guest accommodations located above. This 213-room boutique hotel, like the shops around it, targets a high-end client base that is willing to pay a premium for luxury services. Directly behind the Hotel Valencia lies another outdoor area, the Plaza di Valencia. Sporting a water feature, this park is bordered on two sides by a variety of restaurants.

The optimal placement of buildings and the uses within them was based on buildings' connections to the streets, views, parking, and access, as well as the need to create a sense of privacy and security. There also had to be a synergy among parks, open space, and structures, which would support the holistic concept of Santana Row as more than a kit of unrelated parts. The members of the development team adhered to four distinct strategies to help guide them:

The development team attempted to use the retail spaces to give the streets a sense of rhythm. Federal Realty carefully selected tenants and placed them in strategic locations. Anchor stores, entertainment venues, and the hotel were each located in places with great visual prominence, maximal parking, and auto and foot circulation. Three of the main anchor

Santana Row Park features fountains, an oversized chess board, and vendors selling wares from carts.

Photograph by Jennifer LeFurgy

stores are located along Stevens Creek Boulevard, giving them the highest exposure to automobile traffic. Along the main street sit most of the high-end luxury shops, while the independent, smaller shops and convenience-oriented retail stores are mostly located along Olsen Drive and Olin Avenue.

Noting that residential uses add life to streets, the development team placed them in locations where they would have the strongest effect on the street life. Loft units, commonly associated with high-density urban living, were placed in the most urban location in Santana Row. The location of the Villa Cornet, home of the most expensive and well-appointed units in Santana Row, is located in the center of the project, which is directly across from the Hotel Valencia. The townhouses are located at the edges of the project and along the less-busy side streets, giving residents more privacy and quiet.

Federal Realty used parks and restaurants as gathering spots. The two most popular outdoor public gathering places are Santana Row Park and Plaza di Valencia, both of which feature a vari-

The lounge area attracts visitors with comfortable chairs, sun umbrellas, and a fire pit.

Photograph by Jennifer LeFurgy

ety of seating accommodations, activities, and uses. By design, the greatest concentration of restaurants can be found grouped around each of these parks. Other restaurants are located throughout the development in order to energize every block, with the fewest in the luxury shopping area according to the merchants' request.

Parking was an important part of the design strategy for the development team, and they believed that parking could support all uses and contribute to the pedestrian experience. Each building was designed to promote pedestrian activity and to conceal its parking. This concealment is accomplished differently on every block. The majority of parking is located in garages that are ringed with retail space, are found underground, or are raised on top of a podium. Surface lots also occupy future development sites. Visitor parking is easy to locate, whereas resident parking is accessed from secondary streets. Parallel parking along all the streets buffers the sidewalks and promotes their use for dining, strolling, and shopping. Service areas tucked behind buildings are accessed from side streets and lanes to reduce conflict.

All residential rental units were designed for easy conversion to condominiums.

Photograph by Jennifer LeFurgy

Architectural details and building components were designed with the goal of optimizing the pedestrian experience. The aesthetics of Santana Row's entire physical environment are governed by a set of urban design guidelines and architectural standards that are developed specifically for the project. Intentionally, these were not overly detailed to encourage original and creative exterior design solutions, especially for the retail façades and gallerias.

The Future of Santana Row and Lessons Learned

In 2004, the Santa Row CineArts Theater opened as a venue for independent movies in a state-of-the-art facility. The developer is preparing for the construction of the first new building in several years: an eight-level wholly residential structure on a parking lot behind the Serrano Building. The new addition will contain 238 rental or ownership units on a parcel currently containing 264 parking spaces.

Santana Row stands as a modern-day leader in town center development. Not only did the project prevail despite several economic downtowns and a fire, but also the development team and the city created model codes for an ever-expanding niche: higher-density suburban infill projects. Moreover, it is one of the most fully realized and beautifully designed examples of the town center concept.

Federal Realty plans to continue doing mixed-use projects, but with a slightly different approach. The following are a few things the REIT learned in the process of executing such an ambitious concept on its own:

☐ **REDUCE FINANCIAL RISK** by partnering with government entities, private developers, or both.

☐ **PHASE DEVELOPMENT** to capitalize on equity and momentum; allow change over time in response to shifting markets; control cost; and simplify construction management.

☐ **ANTICIPATE REFINEMENT OF IDEAS AND DETAILS** as the project matures and the learning curve flattens.

☐ **MAINTAIN CLARITY** of the relationships between uses at all times.

☐ **SHOPPING STREETS** need variety to remain vital and to "mix things up." Grouping luxury tenants in one area without restaurants was not ideal. Creating a livelier street scene where uses are more integrated would have been better.

☐ **THE CREATION OF A SUPERIOR STREET EXPERIENCE** establishes significant value for all uses. In this kind of environment, residential tenants will pay a premium to have a unit overlooking the street as opposed to other views.

☐ **PLAN FOR THE FUTURE.** In this case, condo-mapping all the residential units provides an exit strategy for Federal Realty with respect to ownership of the residential component.

Wide sidewalks and attractive lighting help create a lively pedestrian atmosphere in the evenings.

Photograph by Jennifer LeFurgy

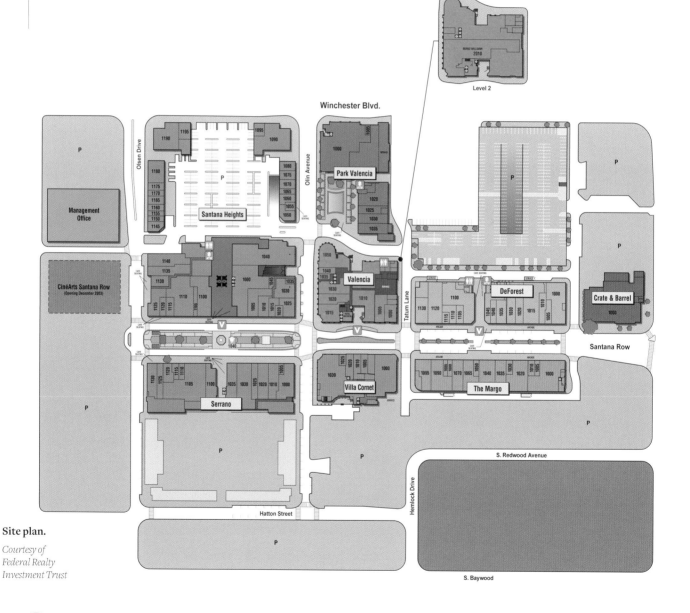

Santana Row

SAN JOSE, CALIFORNIA

www.santanarow.com

Level 2

Winchester Blvd.

Olsen Drive

Olin Avenue

1195 · 1190 · 1095 · 1090

1180

1175 · 1170 · 1165 · 1160 · 1155 · 1150 · 1145

Santana Heights

1080 · 1075 · 1070 · 1065 · 1060 · 1055 · 1050

P

CAFE SEATING

1095 · 1005

1000

Park Valencia

1020 · 1025 · 1030 · 1035

CAFE SEATING

BURKE WILLIAMS 2010

Management Office

CinéArts Santana Row
(Opening December 2003)

P

P

P

1140 · 1135 · 1130

1040

1125 · 1120 · 1115 · 1110 · 1106 · 1100 · 1000 · 1045 · 1095 · 1010 · 1015 · 1020 · 1025

1035 · 1030

CAFE SEATING

1050 · 1040 · 1035 · 1030 · 1020 · 1015

Valencia

1010 · 1006 · 1005 · 1000

Tatum Lane

SERVICE · SERVICE

1130 · 1120 · 1115 · 1110 · 1105 · 1100

1045 · 1040 · 1035 · 1030 · 1020 · 1015 · 1005

DeForest

1010 · 1000

CAFE SEATING

Crate & Barrel

1000

P

1040

CAFE SEATING

1130 · 1125 · 1120 · 1115 · 1110 · 1105 · 1100

1035 · 1030 · 1020 · 1010 · 1005 · 1000

Serrano

1025 · 1010 · 1005 · 1000

1030

Villa Cornet

ARCADE

1095 · 1090 · 1085 · 1080 · 1070 · 1065 · 1060 · 1040 · 1035 · 1020 · 1010 · 1005 · 1000

The Margo

ARCADE · ARCADE

Santana Row

P

S. Redwood Avenue

Hemlock Drive

P

P

Hatton Street

S. Baywood

Site plan.

Courtesy of Federal Realty Investment Trust

PROJECT TYPE

Town Center/Urban Village on a Redevelopment Site
Single Owner
Site area: 42 acres/17 hectares

LAND USE

Use	Square Feet	Number of Establishments/Units
Retail:	563,000	106
Residential (rentals, condos, and primary residences):		529
Hotel:		213
Parking:		4,000
Transit Linkages:		Bus

DEVELOPMENT COSTS

Site Acquisition Cost:	$55,000,000
Total Town Center/Urban Village Development Cost:	$532,000,000

DEVELOPMENT SCHEDULE

Planning Began:	March 1997
Ground Breaking:	June 2001
Phase I Complete:	November 2002
Phase II Complete:	February 2003
Phase III Complete:	August 2004
Phase IV Complete:	January 2006

DEVELOPMENT TEAM

Developer:
Federal Realty Investment Trust
Rockville, Maryland
www.federalrealty.com

Owner:
Federal Realty Investment Trust
Rockville, Maryland
www.federalrealty.com

Master Planner:
Street-Works
White Plains, New York
www.street-works.com

Architects:
SB Architects
San Francisco, California
www.sandybabcock.com

Backen Arrigoni and Ross
(BAR Architects)
San Francisco, California
www.bararch.com

MBH Architects
Alameda, California
www.mbharch.com

Landscape Architect:
The SWA Group
San Francisco, California
www.swagroup.com

Place Making and Environmental Design:
Maestri Design, Inc.
Seattle, Washington
www.maestridesign.com

Residential Consultant:
Group Interland Management
San Mateo, California
www.interlandusa.com

Construction Management:
Bovis Lend Lease, Inc.
San Francisco, California
www.bovislendlease.com

South Campus Gateway

COLUMBUS, OHIO

South Campus Gateway represents a significant first step in the revitalization of the High Street corridor, which runs along the main campus of the Ohio State University (OSU) and was historically a commercial core for the city of Columbus, Ohio. Although the area had been marred by crime and dilapidated buildings, it is now a center of 24/7 activity. As a $153 million, seven-building, mixed-use entertainment complex, the South Campus Gateway is located on the southern edge of the Columbus campus and is the result of an almost ten-year partnership between the city and the university. The project's five-story structures contain restaurants and nightspots, an eight-screen arts cinema, a 50,000-square-foot (5,000-square-meter) campus bookstore, a 14,000-square-foot (1,300-square-meter) natural foods grocery store, several locally and nationally owned boutique shops, 184 market-rate apartments, 88,000 square feet (8,000 square meters) of office space, and a 1,200-space parking garage.

The central pedestrian alley provides a popular place to linger and is the location of the theater and outdoor seating for restaurants.

Photo by Brad Feinkopf

The Revitalization of a District

South Campus Gateway was designed not only to make a visual effect on the southern entrance to Ohio State's campus, but also to spur future redevelopment and revitalization along the entire High Street corridor and its adjacent neighborhoods. As universities across the country begin to take a renewed interest in revitalizing their urban surroundings, South Campus Gateway provides a template for how to shape redevelopment along the edge of a large urban campus.

By the early 1990s, the south campus area had seriously deteriorated after decades of disinvestment. Because it is located in a federally designated empowerment zone and is, therefore, eligible for business tax credits and other incentives that are dedicated to economic development, the municipal and university officials took advantage of those and other financial mechanisms to clean up the area, to improve the adjacent neighborhoods, and to stimulate private investment. To that end, the city and university teamed up in 1995 to form Campus Partners for Community Urban Redevelopment to lead in efforts to revitalize the University District. A nonprofit organization that is closely affiliated with the university, Campus Partners acts as the coordinating entity among the

168

city; the university; and the various stakeholders, neighborhood groups, and citizens who are interested in revitalizing the area.

Campus Partners led a multiyear public planning process to develop a plan for the 2.5-mile (4.0-kilometer) stretch of High Street in the University District. The first major project in the implementation process was the construction of South Campus Gateway, which was seen as an opportunity to build an urban infill project that would benefit the immediate area and serve as a catalyst for revitalization in the surrounding neighborhoods and elsewhere along the High Street corridor.

South Campus Gateway was the result of a partnership between the city of Columbus and the Ohio State University. Pathways directly connect the campus to the development.

Photo by Brad Feinkopf

Planning and Design

The overarching goal for South Campus Gateway was to create a destination for both on-campus and off-campus users. To reach the goal, Campus Partners needed to attract anchors and a range of dining and retail options that previously had not existed on High Street. Campus Partners felt it was critical to build a project that would create value and encourage further private investment in the revitalization of the High Street corridor and its adjacent neighborhoods. To achieve this vital support, the design team placed a strong emphasis on several key urban design principles.

Buildings are constructed on the sidewalk edge with a strong orientation to, and engagement of, the street. The project's sidewalks are intended to provide a pleasant experience and to allow space for outdoor dining. On-street parking is provided (at some loss in net leasable space) to help mitigate the effects of vehicular traffic on the five-lane High Street corridor. The 1,200-space parking structure is behind the buildings, is hidden from High Street, and is screened from adjacent residential streets by three-story residential structures. Buildings are scaled to frame the street and are designed to connect with, but not to mimic, the surrounding urban fabric. Retail storefronts are not constructed as part of the core and shell, but rather they are the obligation of the retail tenants (with appropriate design review) to express their brand and to provide design diversity along the street.

South Campus Gateway comprises seven new buildings that are located within three city blocks. It reestablishes the urban grid, which had been disrupted by one-way and closed-off streets. Gateway's three retail anchors are designed and scaled to fit in with the overall project and are placed throughout the site to have maximal effect. Sunflower Market, a natural foods grocery store, is located at the southern end of the project; the Gateway Theater occupies the interior of the pedestrian alley; and the Barnes & Noble/OSU bookstore is placed at High Street and East 11th Avenue—one of the project's most prominent corners. A fourth anchor that was not in the original plans has also emerged on the north end of the project: Eddie George's Grille 27, which is a sports-themed restaurant in which former OSU football star Eddie George has a stake. The dining establishment has been an attraction for alumni and other patrons from across Columbus.

As mentioned previously, the five-story garage is hidden behind the main complex and is fronted on two sides with three-story apartment buildings that contain a total of 26 units. The main entrance to the parking garage has a glass elevator structure and spills out to a pedestrian alley that runs through the heart of the project. As part of the original design concept of the Druker Company and Elkus Manfredi Architects, this public space is home to the movie theater; boutique retail; and several bars, nightclubs, and restaurants with outdoor seating areas. Two of the bars and nightclubs have second-story balconies that overlook the pedestrian alley and add a third dimension to the public space.

The pedestrian alley features special LED and fiber-optic lighting, seating made from granite, street trees, and other streetscape elements to create a gathering place that is Gateway's locus of activity, especially during evening hours. Various retail and restaurant establishments that have outdoor seating and transparent façades occupy the remainder of the High Street frontage and are intended to activate the street and to stimulate interest from passersby. An additional 158 apartments occupy the upper levels of structures fronting High Street, and an 88,000-square-foot (8,000-square-meter) office space is concentrated on the three upper floors of the Barnes & Noble building.

At significant expense, overhead utility lines were buried as part of the city's infrastructure improvements. Narrow sidewalks were replaced with ones that are 15 feet to 22 feet (4.6 meters to 6.7 meters) wide and that accommodate street furnishings and outdoor dining areas. The furnishings include steel bike racks that complement the streetlights and trash cans. All streetlights and street trees are aligned with the building columns to ensure that storefronts are visible and that the sidewalk is comfortable for pedestrians.

Daytime and evening activity is supported through uses such as a campus bookstore, a natural foods grocery, restaurants, and upscale nightclubs.

Photo by Brad Feinkopf

A run-down stretch of deteriorated buildings has been replaced with a vibrant urban village.

Photo by Brad Feinkopf

Mature street trees were chosen to further reduce the effect on storefront visibility and to provide more immediate shade for the sidewalks. Other efforts to create an uncluttered streetscape included combining streetlights with stoplight posts at intersections. Campus Partners also opted to improve the city-standard sodium vapor light fixture with white metal halide fixtures to provide a more aesthetically pleasing environment.

The architecture of South Campus Gateway represents an increase in the scale and density of the neighborhood while responding to its historic urban context. Each building has a distinct bottom, middle, and top. The retail frontages have traditional bay widths and ground-level materials that are intended to be reminiscent of a traditional Main Street. Facades are transparent and entrances are easy to find. However, there are modern touches. Although stone and brick are the predominant building materials, differentiated materials and architectural elements define building entrances and façades. The upper stories of the three- to five-story structures feature a large amount of glass and metal to lend a more contemporary take on a traditional building style. Even though the project is somewhat denser than the surrounding neighborhood, Campus Partners believes that in the next 20 or 30 years, South Campus Gateway will blend in seamlessly with other developments as similar building types are encouraged to replace the older structures.

Tenant Mix

Campus Partners conceived of South Campus Gateway as a project that not only would serve university students, but also would meet the needs of nearby residents, workers, and faculty members and would attract visitors from across Columbus. With that in mind, Campus Partners sought to make Gateway a regional destination. The movie theater, which is one of only a handful in the area showing art films, is intended to be a significant draw, as are the restaurants, many of which are unique to the Columbus market.

Campus Partners decided not to build undergraduate housing or to cater to that market and instead erected higher-end units that would appeal to graduate students and young professionals. A significant portion of the residences are occupied by law students from Ohio State's nearby Moritz College of Law. Other residents include OSU faculty and staff members, owners and managers of Gateway businesses, and individuals who are simply attracted to the mixed-use environment. As of June 2007, the apartments were 100 percent leased, and rates average $1.15 per square foot. Office space is 78 percent leased and is occupied entirely by OSU uses.

The merchandising mix of Gateway is approximately one-third anchors (Barnes & Noble, Sunflower Market, and the Gateway cinema); one-third by restaurants and bars; and one-third by apparel, service, and general retail businesses. The overarching retailing strategy for South Campus Gateway was to provide products that previously were not available in the University District. Because there is a plethora of fast-food establishments along the rest of High Street in the University District, Campus Partners decided to focus on sit-down restaurants. The bars and nightclubs at the project tend to be trendy and upscale.

Upscale rental units above the ground-level retail have helped spur reinvestment in nearby apartment buildings.

Photo by Brad Feinkopf

With the intention of maintaining the project's distinctiveness in the area market, as well as its Main Street character, Campus Partners is committed to incubating local startup businesses in addition to attracting established local and national brands. For example, Campus Partners has helped both a bath and beauty boutique and a restaurant concept, which were developed by two recent OSU graduates, get off the ground by providing financial and other assistance.

Influence on the Area

As the development team had anticipated, the overall effect of South Campus Gateway is reaching beyond the confines of the redevelopment site. Apartments and other structures that were previously dilapidated are now being fixed up because landlords and other property owners are taking advantage of the increasing desirability of the location. The completion of the project has given Campus Partners the credibility it needs to tackle additional redevelopment within the community.

South Campus Gateway

COLUMBUS, OHIO

www.southcampusgateway.com

Site plan.

*Courtesy of
Elkus Manfredi Architects*

PROJECT TYPE

Urban Village on a Redevelopment Site
Single Owner
Site Area: 7.5 acres/3.0 hectares

LAND USE

Use	Square Feet	Number of Establishments/Units
Office:	88,000	6
Retail:	249,000	23
Residential (rental):	205,000	184
Parking:	390,000	1,200
Transit Linkages:		Bus

DEVELOPMENT COSTS

Site Acquisition Cost:	$20,000,000
Site Improvement Cost:	$9,639,212
Soft Costs:	$47,813,710
Construction Costs:	$82,452,266
Total Urban Village Development Cost:	$159,905,188

DEVELOPMENT SCHEDULE

Planning Began:	2000
Ground Breaking:	2003
Town Center/Urban Village Buildout:	2005

DEVELOPMENT TEAM

Developer:
Campus Partners
Columbus, Ohio
www.campuspartners.osu.edu

Master Planner:
Goody Clancy
Boston, Massachusetts
www.goodyclancy.com

Architect:
Elkus Manfredi Architects
Boston, Massachusetts
www.elkus-manfredi.com

Development Manager:
Jones Lang LaSalle
McLean, Virginia
www.joneslanglasalle.com

Construction Contractor:
Turner Construction
Worthington, Ohio
www.turnerconstruction.com

Engineer:
EMH&T
Columbus, Ohio
www.emht.com

SouthSide Works

PITTSBURGH, PENNSYLVANIA

SouthSide Works is a pedestrian-oriented urban village that consists of retail shops, restaurants, offices, apartments, and a cinema that are oriented around a central square and a landscaped open space in Pittsburgh's historic South Side neighborhood. Located on a 37.2-acre (15.1-hectare) brownfield redevelopment site that is approximately 1.5 miles (2.4 kilometers) from Pittsburgh's central business district (CBD) and that had previously been occupied by an LTV Steel mill, the project extends the scale of a vibrant historic neighborhood to the city's underused riverfront, while incorporating ample green space.

As of June 2007, the project comprised 525,000 square feet (49,000 square meters) of Class A office space, 288,000 square feet (27,000 square meters) of retail and entertainment space including a ten-screen movie theater, 83 units of flats and loft-style apartments, 6.5 acres (2.6 hectares) of green space, four parking garages, and a temporary surface parking lot. The retail and restaurant tenants are a mix of local establishments and national chains. At buildout, SouthSide Works will feature a boutique hotel, two riverfront condominium towers, three additional office towers, and an outdoor performance venue.

Postindustrial Place Making

In recent years, the city of Pittsburgh has attempted to reposition its economy as postindustrial, focusing its economic development efforts on retaining young people, knowledge workers, and other members of the "creative class." One of its recent repositioning strategies has been the redevelopment of former industrial sites for job creation and economic development. The development of SouthSide Works is an example of this strategy.

SouthSide Works's site had been occupied by a succession of steel mills for nearly 150 years. In 1854, Benjamin Franklin Jones and James Laughlin founded a company that would later become known as J&L (Jones & Laughlin) Steel on the site. The adjacent South Side Flats neighborhood was the late 19th-century home to many steel workers. In 1968, LTV Steel purchased J&L Steel. The plant closed in 1986 because of increased foreign competition, high labor costs, and

technological obsolescence, and the property was abandoned. The South Side Flats neighborhood fell into economic and physical decline during the second half of the 20th century as the city's industry waned.

Pittsburgh's Urban Redevelopment Authority (URA) purchased the abandoned 110-acre (44.5-hectare) LTV property in 1993 and began master planning efforts, hiring Boston–based Sasaki Associates. Sasaki's plan broke the site into parcels, including the 37.2-acre (15.1-hectare) parcel that would eventually become the site of SouthSide Works. As of June 2007, the balance of the original 110-acre (44.5-hectare) site is home to University of Pittsburgh Medical Center spin-offs, the International Brotherhood of Electrical Workers, the FBI, and football practice fields that are used by the Pittsburgh Steelers. The western edge of the original site contains 270 apartments that were developed in 2003 by the Continental Real Estate Companies of Columbus, Ohio.

In 1996, after a request for qualifications (RFQ) process, the Soffer Organization, a locally based real estate company, was awarded the development rights to the 37.2-acre (15.1-hectare) parcel of the larger site that would become SouthSide Works. The two entities entered a public/private partnership to develop SouthSide Works. The Soffer Organization advocated a neotraditional configuration for the project, and in 1997, the city created a special zoning district to allow for such a concept. The city was responsible for the costs of infrastructure, environmental remedia-

The building materials and scale were designed to complement the fabric of the adjacent neighborhoods.

Courtesy of the Soffer Organization

tion, and parking. In addition to development costs, Soffer was deemed to be responsible for prior use–related cleanup, which consisted primarily of removing subsurface infrastructure. Tax increment financing (TIF) was used to pay for the infrastructure upgrades that were necessary for the redevelopment of the larger 110-acre (44.5-hectare) site.

The site's prior industrial use posed obstacles to redevelopment. First, it was a brownfield, which required substantial environmental cleanup and was embedded with steel mill foundations that had to be removed before any significant rebuilding could take place. The remediation process consisted primarily of soil cleanup, because there was no groundwater contamination on the prop-

SouthSide
Works—a
mixed-use
urban village—
is located on a
former steel
mill site.

*Photograph by
Walter Larrimore*

erty. Running parallel to the river, an operational cut-and-cover rail line bisects the site, and because no structures can be built on the train tunnel lid, the rail line provided an opportunity to create a linear green space through the development.

Extension and Enhancement of East Carson Street

The project was designed to complement the extant historic fabric of the adjacent neighborhoods. East Carson Street, a National Register–listed historic district, is lined with late 19th-century, low-rise, mercantile buildings. East Carson Street, which still serves as the main business artery for the

South Side of Pittsburgh, is part of a larger grid of 19th-century streets where adjoining two- to four-story brick structures are the predominant building pattern.

Accordingly, the structures at SouthSide Works complement their historic environs in scale and building materials. The mixed-use urban village's East Carson Street buildings are in a flush row with existing structures, thereby extending the street wall. SouthSide Works's buildings are low rise and mimic the massing of those of their immediate context. Many of the buildings—particularly those that face outward—are made of brick, and the closer the buildings are to the river, the more they incorporate glass and steel. However, the structures at SouthSide Works lack excessive nostalgia. Many of them have modern flourishes that unobtrusively distinguish them from the area's historic building stock while serving as gentle reminders of the site's industrial past. Although the project was master planned by Development Design Group, individual structures were designed by different architects. The result is eclectic and urban. The street grid by SouthSide Works is integrated with that of the neighborhood, producing a functional and stylistic continuity between the old neighborhood and the new development.

Open space is a major component of SouthSide Works. The South Side's historic development pattern left little open space for recreation, and community stakeholders asked that substantial open space be included in the project's plan. SouthSide Works is oriented around a town square, which reads as the project's center and lies just a block from the East Carson Street commercial corridor. The South Side riverfront trail network, which is part of a wider trail system that connects all the way to Washington, D.C., passes through the site. Because it cannot be built on, the land above the operational rail tunnel is developed as a landscaped 3-acre (1.2-hectare) park. The landscaping plan for the project makes use of indigenous plantings, which reduces irrigation needs and requires minimal maintenance.

Left: A fountain in the town square serves as entertainment and as a place to relax; the open space between the Quantum I building and one of the parking garages contains a large iron sculpture representing Pittsburgh's three rivers.

Courtesy of the Soffer Organization

Live, Work, and Play for the Creative Class

SouthSide Works's speculative office buildings were constructed with university research and spin-off companies in mind, given the site's proximity to Oakland, which is the city's burgeoning technology center and is home to both Carnegie Mellon University and the University of Pittsburgh. Both universities are located about 2 miles (3.2 kilometers) from the project. Analyses conducted early in the development process indicated that roughly two-thirds of traffic to SouthSide Works would come across the refurbished Hot Metal Bridge, which connects the South Side to downtown Pittsburgh. Because East Carson Street was the existing artery through the neighborhood, the project development phasing began at that corner site. The Quantum I office building, the project's first structure, was erected at that intersection. Further development emanated from the intersection.

Oakland's incubator space is considered to be saturated, and many more established technology and medical-based companies have been searching elsewhere for sites. Quantum I, SouthSide Works's first speculative office building, was fully leased to the University of Pittsburgh Medical Center. In 2005, Quantum II, SouthSide Works's second office building, was purchased by American Eagle Outfitters, which moved its corporate headquarters to the site in June 2007.

Targeting a variety of users, including the academic community, professionals, tourists, and area residents, SouthSide Work's live/work/play environment is particularly intended to serve the creative class, which Pittsburgh hopes to attract and retain for its economic repositioning as a service-based economy. To that end, the urban village features a variety of "third places" such as coffee shops, a bookstore, a cinema, restaurants, and riverfront recreation venues. The retail tenant mix comprises both local establishments and national retailers, many of which are new to the Pittsburgh market. Nearly all of the retail space, with notable exceptions such as REI and Cheesecake Factory, was built speculatively. As of June 2007, SouthSide Works had 46 retailers, the entire site south of the rail line had been developed, and plans are underway for the northern portion of the site.

In the past decade, the South Side Flats neighborhood has seen something of a renaissance, becoming a chic and diverse area with businesses ranging from fine dining establishments to tattoo parlors to antique shops. SouthSide Works was developed with the intention of building on this momentum.

Wide sidewalks with seating frame the town square, which is located one block from the historic district of East Carson Street.

Courtesy of the Soffer Organization

SouthSide Works

PITTSBURGH, PENNSYLVANIA
www.southsideworks, com

Site plan.

Courtesy of the
Soffer Organization

PROJECT TYPE

Town Center/Urban Village on a Redevelopment Site
Separate Owners
Site Area: 37.2 acres /15.1 hectares

LAND USE

Use	Square Feet	Number of Establishments/Units
Office:	524,860	
Retail:	288,143	
Residential (rental):		83
Parking:		2,426
Transit Linkages:		Bus

DEVELOPMENT COSTS

Total Development Cost: $208,700,000

DEVELOPMENT SCHEDULE

Planning Began:	1995
Ground Breaking:	1996
Project Opened:	2002
Town Center/Urban Village Buildout:	TBD

DEVELOPMENT TEAM

Developers:

South Side Local Development Company
Pittsburgh, Pennsylvania
www.southsidepgh.com

The Soffer Organization
Pittsburgh, Pennsylvania
www.sofferorganization.com

Master Planners:

Development Design Group, Inc.
Baltimore, Maryland
www.ddg-usa.com

Environmental Planning & Design, LLC
Pittsburgh, Pennsylvania
www.epd-pgh.com

Public Partner:

Urban Redevelopment Authority of
Pittsburgh
Pittsburgh, Pennsylvania
www.ura.org

183

Victoria Gardens

RANCHO CUCAMONGA, CALIFORNIA

Situated at the foothills of the San Bernardino Mountains in southern California's burgeoning Inland Empire, Victoria Gardens is a pedestrian-oriented town center that integrates department stores, shops, restaurants, a movie theater, a children's library and cultural center, housing, and offices around a town square. Forest City, a national development company, and the Lewis Group of Companies, a local developer, formed a public/private partnership with the Rancho Cucamonga Redevelopment Agency to create Victoria Gardens, which, when completed, will comprise more than 2.4 million square feet (223,000 square meters) of space.

The project's detailed, historically inspired design is based on a postmodern storyboard for how a southern California downtown might have organically evolved from a modest grouping of agricultural structures along a farm road into Main Street buildings that are designed in art deco, moderne, and contemporary styles.

The city of Rancho Cucamonga, Forest City, and the Lewis Group of Companies formed a public/private partnership to develop Victoria Gardens.

RMA Photography

A Place-Making Partnership

At the time of its incorporation in 1977, the city of Rancho Cucamonga recognized the need for a focal point to create an identity for the community. The agricultural fields at the intersection of Interstate 15 (I-15) and Foothill Boulevard were identified by the Rancho Cucamonga Redevelopment Agency as being ripe for such development, which was then envisioned as an enclosed shopping mall. The land was under agreement with a private developer to be developed as an enclosed mall between 1983 and 1997, but that deal failed as a result of the significant costs for regional-serving infrastructure, the corporate mergers in the retail industry, and the recession of the early 1990s. In 1997, the land was returned to the city.

In early 1999, the city reissued a request for qualifications to develop a two-story enclosed regional shopping mall on the site. In September 1999, the city selected the partnership between Forest City and the Lewis Group for exclusive negotiations with the city to create a mall.

From the outset, public assistance was critical to the viability of the project. Creative approaches to financing, such as the use of a community facilities district, which allows for financing of public

improvements and services, were used to make the needed infrastructure improvements. The city of Rancho Cucamonga transferred the project site to Forest City for $1. In return for the land subsidy, a look-back calculation will be made four years after the center's opening; if audited cost and income data show that the developer is achieving a return on cost that is higher than the target, there will be a partial repayment of the land subsidy. Additionally, the Rancho Cucamonga Redevelopment Agency is entitled to a share of excess proceeds from the sale or refinancing of the project if the proceeds are in excess of audited total development costs for the first sale or refinancing and in excess of the increased basis from sale or refinancing.

A New Focal Point within a Sprawling Community

Historically a center for citrus production, the farmlands in much of Rancho Cucamonga were bought up by homebuilders in the 1970s and were largely developed into lower-cost, low-intensity subdivisions as southern California's urban envelope expanded. Located 50 miles (80.5

kilometers) east of downtown Los Angeles, the Victoria Gardens site occupies a 175-acre (70.8-hectare) parcel of land at the intersection of I-15 and Foothill Boulevard in the affluent suburb of Rancho Cucamonga, in the heart of the Inland Empire. Victoria Gardens is bounded on the north by single-family houses, on the west by both single-family homes and multifamily housing, on the south by Foothill Boulevard (one of the primary east-west arterials in the area), and on the east by I-15.

As plans for the mall evolved, Forest City recognized a need to differentiate it from nearby retail competition and to create a new focal point in the heart of an existing community. Accordingly, plans for the mall evolved into a pedestrian-friendly, open-air, mixed-use design, which was the first of its kind in the Inland Empire. The city also incorporated civic uses into the project, forming a mixed-use town center. The project serves as a new model for higher-density, mixed-use development in a region of southern California that has been characterized by low-density, land-consumptive sprawl.

Forest City recognized that changing demographics were creating an emerging opportunity at the eastern end of the Inland Empire. However, persuading retailers to locate in the project proved to be a challenge. As is commonly an issue with place-making projects, potential retail tenants

The imagined urban history of the site was not intended to fake a historic setting but rather to add texture, color, and interest to the project.

RMA Photography

were concerned about the lack of prominent street signs or streetfront visibility from a major arterial. For retailers, one upside to the location was the draw of the civic uses—the library and the performing arts center—that are projected to be used by 500,000 people annually when they are completed. However, it was Forest City's strong relationships with national retailers that secured tenants that were "on the fence." After a few key national tenants were secured, including Talbots, Williams-Sonoma, and Pottery Barn, other retailers followed. Today, Victoria Gardens comprises more than 120 stores, including Macy's and JCPenney department stores.

Historically Inspired, Richly Textured

Victoria Gardens' sense of place is attributable in part to a postmodern notion of an imagined urban history. The master plan, created by San Francisco–based Field Paoli, is based on an elaborate fictional storyboard for how a downtown might have organically developed in Rancho Cucamonga—from a modest grouping of agricultural buildings along a farm road into civic and commercial structures that had been erected in a range of architectural styles. Victoria Gardens is configured according to a traditional street grid built to a pedestrian scale.

The result of the imagined history concept is an eclectic mix of buildings with differentiated and often dissonant styles designed by four architecture firms—Field Paoli, Elkus Manfredi, Altoon + Porter, and KA Architecture. Each street has a different feel, further contributing to the notion of a place that might have evolved over time. Street widths are varied and sidewalks are paved with 12

The design concept emphasizes a mix of buildings with a range of differentiated and often dissonant architectural styles.

Photo by Tom Fox, SWA Group

Freestanding kiosks keep pedestrian traffic flowing between retailers.

Photo by Tom Fox, SWA Group

different surfaces. Plantings and other landscaping details are similarly varied. In addition, preexisting slopes throughout the site were not leveled during construction. The signature edifice at Victoria Gardens is its food hall, which was designed to be reminiscent of a citrus packing house from the early 1900s. Buildings evoking craftsman, mission, and Spanish colonial styles are located along the adjacent North Mainstreet, while the town square is surrounded by civic-looking structures that mimic the neoclassical style. The buildings of South Mainstreet—where the department stores are located—evoke streamlined modernist styles, ranging from moderne to art deco. Individual buildings were named after early settlers of the area; examples include Kilbourn Hall, the L.M. Hold Building, and two structures named after the Chaffey brothers (two of the area's first Anglo settlers). The vast majority of the retail space in Victoria Gardens is single story; in retrospect, officials at Forest City say that they might have considered multistory buildings that incorporated residential units on levels above the retail uses. This design would have increased synergies between residential and retail uses, as well as improving streetscape aesthetics.

It is important to mention that Victoria Gardens clearly reads as a new project; it is not an attempt to fake a historic cluster of buildings. The storyboarding and interpretation of a downtown that may have evolved over time are intended only to add texture, color, and interest to the project.

The project also includes numerous fountains and other water features, which are intended to link its design with the nearby mountain waters. Paseos, pocket parks, and courtyards connect the main streets and the parking areas. Salvaged neon signs, tiled pavements, murals, and building plaques telling the history of Rancho Cucamonga contribute to the imagined layers of Victoria Gardens.

One challenge was parking. The vast surface parking lots necessary to support this project were incongruous with the pedestrian-oriented streetscape of a true downtown, so three parking garages were built. As of May 2007, the center had more than 5,600 parking spaces split between surface lots and structured facilities. Currently, the development is almost entirely surrounded by surface parking lots, but the project is entitled for almost 1 million more square feet (93,000 square meters) of development. It is anticipated that buildings will occupy many of those parking fields in the near term, and additional new parking structures will be constructed as development proceeds.

Only time will tell how the project's seemingly incremental design ages. One major benefit is that the site consists of many individual buildings, which means that they may be replaced one by one, allowing the project to actually become a downtown that has evolved over time.

Numerous paseos, pocket parks, and courtyards connect the main streets and the parking areas.

Photo by Tom Fox, SWA Group

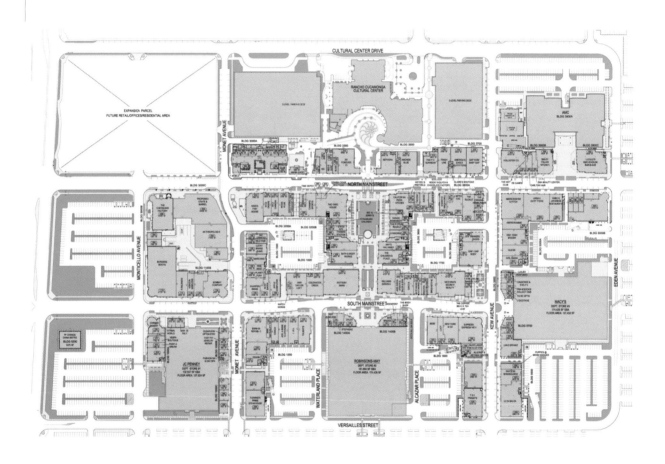

Victoria Gardens

RANCHO CUCAMONGA, CALIFORNIA

www.victoriagardensie.com

Retail site plan.

*Courtesy of Forest
City Commercial
Development*

PROJECT TYPE

Town Center on a Vacant Site
Separate Owners
Site Area: 175 acres/70.8 hectares

LAND USE

Use	Square Feet	Number of Establishments/Units
Office:	55,000	7
Retail:	1,500,000	136
Residential:		310
Civic:	56,000	
Parking:		5,600
Transit Linkages:		Bus

DEVELOPMENT COSTS

Site Acquisition Cost: $232,000
Soft Costs: $23,000,000
Construction Costs: $120,000,000
Total Town Center Development Cost: $128,532,000

DEVELOPMENT SCHEDULE

Planning Began: August 2000
Ground Breaking: October 2003
Phase I Complete: September 2004
Phase II Complete: September 2007
Phase III Complete: Currently Planning

DEVELOPMENT TEAM

Developers:

Forest City Commercial Development
Los Angeles, California
www.forestcity.net

Lewis Group of Companies
Upland, California
www.lewisop.com

Rancho Cucamonga Redevelopment
Agency
Rancho Cucamonga, California
www.ci.rancho-cucamonga.ca.us/govt
rda_director.htm

Architects:

Altoon + Porter Architects
Los Angeles, California
www.altoonporter.com

Elkus Manfredi Architects
Boston, Massachusetts
www.elkus-manfredi.com

Field Paoli
San Francisco, California
www.fieldpaoli.com

KA Architecture
Cleveland, Ohio
www.kainc.com

JRDV
Oakland, California
http://www.jrdv.com

Zona Rosa

KANSAS CITY, MISSOURI

Named after a neighborhood in Mexico City by the previous owner of the site, Zona Rosa is a new town center that is intended to create a "there" in the Northland, the northern suburbs of Kansas City, Missouri. The developer incorporated traditional urban design principals with internal streets, city blocks, and public spaces. The public spaces for civic and social activities—as well as a collection of restaurants, branded stores, and entertainment in the form of a three-screen cinema and a comedy club venue—serve as anchors. To create a mixed-use space, Phase I of the project includes 532,000 square feet (49,440 square meters) of specialty retail, restaurant, and entertainment and 67,000 square feet (6,225 square meters) of office space. Twenty-five loft-style apartments that rise three stories above retail shops invigorate the town center landscape. This project was the developer's first with residential units, and it was undertaken in house. Phase II, which is scheduled to open in the fall of 2008, will include a three-story, 200,000-square-foot (18,600-square-meter) Dillard's department store; additional retail and residential units; and a 135-room hotel, bringing the project to approximately 1 million square feet (92,900 square meters).

As Yaromir Steiner, chief executive officer of Steiner + Associates, says, "People want shopping environments to give them a 'sense of place.' Their demand for good-feeling spaces is increasing. We're going to go back to development inspired by city blocks that will be convertible to other things."

Zona Rosa, with its shopping districts, parks, and community areas, is intended to survive not only for a few decades, but also for future generations.

Formed in 1993, Steiner + Associates specializes in the design, construction, leasing, and marketing of new town centers and focuses on master planning. The company concentrates on suburban locations; actively incorporates the ideals of the new urbanism; and shares the responsibility for planned public spaces, with the public sector providing public spaces that are attractive, commercially vital, and universally accessible. To achieve those objectives, the company consists of three cooperative divisions that focus on the company's core businesses: development, property

management, and entertainment/animation. Steiner + Associates retains property management responsibility for each development project.

Site and Development Process

When the previous owner, a member of the family that had owned the property for years, became interested in creating a town center in the new urbanist style, this 93-acre (37.6-hectare) tract of land came to the developer's attention. The previous landowner researched projects across the country and contacted the developer after learning about Steiner's Easton Town Center in Columbus, Ohio.

The developer's subsequent evaluation of the market concluded that the conditions in the Northland were ripe for development. The Northland had a scarcity of stores and had relatively few restaurants and entertainment venues—key elements in a new town center. At the time, only one major competitor existed: an enclosed mall in decline that was 4 miles (6.4 kilometers) to the east. The developer also noted projections of strong population growth for the area. At the same time, the focus of retail development in the Northland was shifting from several miles east to the vicinity of the site. A small, upscale, open-air center; a power center; a Super Wal-Mart; and a Lowe's sit across Interstate 29 from the site.

Three levels of residential units sit atop street-level retail.

Courtesy of Steiner + Associates

Planning and Design

The design of the center is based on a street grid, with buildings close to the streets, public parks, and a variety of vertically and horizontally integrated uses. A split boulevard creates islands or blocks that are surrounded by internal streets, allowing for more street fronts, double-loaded streets, and places for public spaces. Zona Rosa has two parks: (a) a town square with a performance stage at one end, a children's pop fountain in the middle, and a restaurant whose veranda overlooks the park at the other; and (b) a children's park with some child-oriented retail stores (children's shoes, ice cream) nearby.

In the event of inclement weather, Zona Rosa includes several shelters. For example, at Barnes & Noble visitors can browse or sit at the café. Dick's Sporting Goods also offers shelter. The first floor of the building occupied by Marshalls contains an open space and a children's play area that is populated with colorful, giant fruit.

To avoid creating space that could accommodate only retail or office uses and thus run the risk of failure if the retail market could not support all the space at some future time, Steiner constructed buildings with the potential for reuse. For example, the second-story office space has 2 feet (0.6 meter) of additional ceiling space so it could be used as retail space in the future. Because of the window placement, the second-story retail space could be used as office space.

Big-box retailers, who are typically hesitant to pay lease premiums to be in the center of an upscale shopping center, are accommodated by second-story space in two central locations. The 25,000-square-foot (2,300-square-meter) DSW and the 50,000-square-foot (4,600-square-meter)

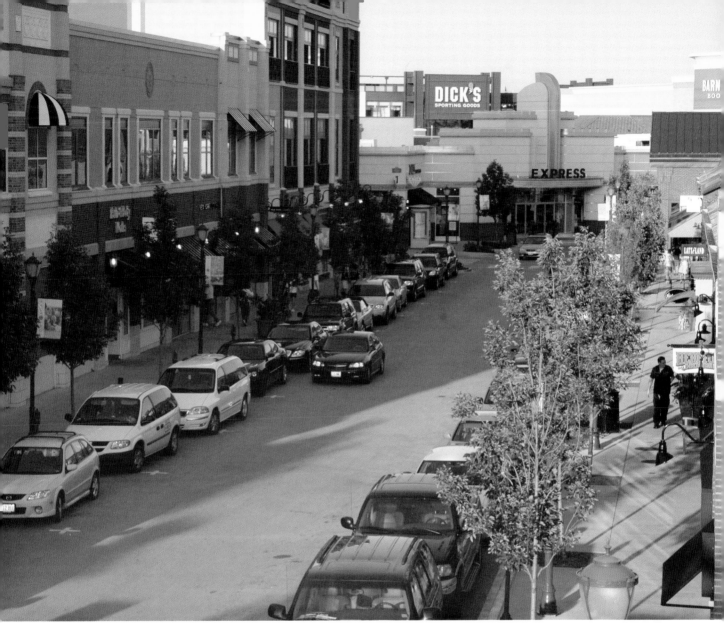

Marshalls 'n More both are accessed by escalators that ascend from two-story spacious lobbies. Other large stores are located on the eastern edge of the town center.

The street that takes visitors into Zona Rosa from Barry Road runs along the long leg of an inverted L. Lining this leg are additional freestanding restaurants, home furnishing and clothing stores, and Gateway Plaza, which is a 30,000-square-foot (2,800-square-meter) retail center that is occupied primarily by service tenants.

Parking is available in a structure on the north perimeter of Phase I, on the surface parking lots that are on all other perimeters, and along on-street metered parallel parking on the internal streets. All off-street parking is free, and the net proceeds from the meters go to charity. The placement of the off-street parking in all directions reduces the size and visual effect of each parking area and allows for easy pedestrian accessibility from all parking areas to the internal streets. The structured parking, while available to all visitors, provides an elevated walkway that goes directly to the resi-

The development was designed to look as though the neighborhood had evolved over time.

Courtesy of Steiner + Associates

dential units and is restricted to residents' use. The total of 2,600 parking spaces exceeds the city's requirement. The number resulted from the developer's calculations, which took into account the variety of uses and when each would be used.

The architectural style of the buildings suggests development over several periods of Kansas City's history. The buildings suggest a street that was reworked through time to form an authentic urban fabric.

Tenants, Marketing, and Management

The leasing team does not lease space simply to fill it. The goal is to ensure that each restaurant, retailer, and entertainment venue that is selected fills a need defined by the community. The team strives to reach a balance among strong national and local retail, restaurant, and entertainment tenants. Although most tenants are major national retailers, the developer is also responsible for the growth of several local small- and medium-sized businesses. Local businesses that opened an additional branch or moved into Zona Rosa include an Indian restaurant, a jewelry store, an Irish pub, and a children's hair-cutting salon. Office tenants include business and medical services such as a law office, a mortgage company, and a dentist.

The residential units are leased through a Web site that allows for online submission of the application form and payment by credit card or directly from the applicant's bank. The Web site provides the layout of each unit that is provided, as well as actual shots of the views from each unit.

The project also includes classrooms for the National American University, a fully accredited university offering a complete range of business degrees and nursing degrees, whose current weekly enrollment is more than 500.

The town square—with features such as a pop fountain and a performance area— draws visitors to its large, open area.

Courtesy of Steiner + Associates

Steiner requires that its management teams seek opportunities to increase revenues from activities other than cost control. Property management teams are responsible for extending the earning power of the property through programs such as marketing and sponsorship agreements.

Marketing and events that promote Zona Rosa as a civic center with community value and function are described as "animation." For example, Steiner revived a Kansas City holiday tradition—a lighting ceremony for holiday crowns. Zona Rosa's holiday crowns are based on the original designs that graced downtown Kansas City from the 1950s to the 1970s. According to Zona Rosa's general manager, "The crowns bring Kansas City back to a time gone by. People can relive their memories while creating a new holiday tradition that they can share with their families."

Each year, Zona Rosa plans to add more crowns to its collection. Events that are held by civic organizations at Zona Rosa receive logistical, staff, and monetary support from the center's management. Zona Rosa also connects with the community through the Zona Rosa Foundation Fund, which receives income through parking meter proceeds and ticket revenues. The fund focuses on providing support to nonprofit organizations in the greater Kansas City area through the Change for Charity Meter Program, the Zona Rosa Scholarship Fund, and community event sponsorships.

The developer has chosen not to place signs with Zona Rosa's name at the site or nearby because the company considers it a place, not a shopping center. It does, however, advertise in places such as hotels where visitors may not know about Zona Rosa. The developer also promotes events in public and tenant spaces, particularly when activities are held in the public space.

Zona Rosa's design is based on a street grid with buildings close to the streets, open space, and mixed uses.

Courtesy of Steiner + Associates

Zona Rosa

KANSAS CITY, MISSOURI

www.zonarosa.com

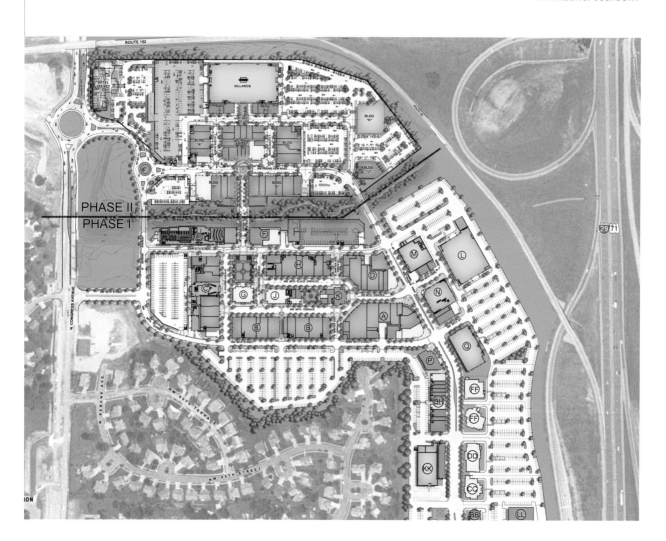

Site plan.

*Courtesy of
Development
Design Group*

PROJECT TYPE

Town Center on a Greenfield Site
Single Owner
Site Area (Phase I):   66 acres /26.7 hectares

LAND USE (PHASE I)

Use	Square Feet	Number of Establishments/Units
Office:	67,000	
Retail:	532,000	
Residential (rental):		25
Parking:		2,600

DEVELOPMENT TEAM

Developer:

Steiner + Associates
Columbus, Ohio
www.steiner.com

Owners:

Steiner + Associates
Columbus, Ohio
www.steiner.com

Mall Properties, Inc.
New York, New York
www.mallproperties.com

Project Architect:

Gould Evans Associates
Kansas City, Missouri
www.gouldevans.com

DEVELOPMENT COSTS (PHASE I)

Site Acquisition Cost:	$16,000,000
Site Improvement Cost:	$11,000,000
Soft Costs:	$28,000,000
Construction Costs:	$66,000,000
Total Town Center Development Cost:	$121,000,000

DEVELOPMENT SCHEDULE

Planning Began:	May 2001
Ground Breaking:	September 2002
Phase I complete:	May 2004
Town Center/Urban Village Buildout:	Fall 2008

Design Architect:

Development Design Group, Inc.
Baltimore, Maryland
www.ddg-usa.com

General Contractor:

Walton Construction
Kansas City, Missouri
www.waltoncci.com